ALL THINGS, SEEN AND UNSEEN

All Things, Seen and Unseen

POEMS: NEW AND
SELECTED, 1967–1997

DAN MASTERSON

The UNIVERSITY of
ARKANSAS PRESS
Fayetteville 1997

BOOKS BY DAN MASTERSON

Pater noster, qui es in coelis: sanctificetur nomen tuum: adveniat regnum tuum: fiat voluntas tua, **sicut** in coelo, **et in terra.** —"Lord's Prayer"

ON EARTH AS IT IS • 1978

Et dimitte nobis debita nostra, sicut et nos **dimittimus debitoribus** nostris. —"Lord's Prayer"

THOSE WHO TRESPASS • 1985

Gloria Patri, et Filio, et Spiritui Sancto. Sicut erat in principio, et nunc, et semper: et in **saecula saeculorum.** —"Gloria"

WORLD WITHOUT END • 1991

Credo in unum Deum, Patrem omnipotentem, factorem coeli et terrae, **visibilium omnium et invisibilium.** —"Nicene Creed"

ALL THINGS, SEEN AND UNSEEN • 1997

Copyright 1997 by Dan Masterson

All rights reserved
Manufactured in the United States

01   00   99   98   97   5   4   3   2   1

Designed by Alice Gail Carter

♾ The paper used in this publication meets the minimum requirements of the American National Standard for Permanence of Paper for Printed Library Materials   Z39.48-1984.

LIBRARY OF CONGRESS CATALOGING-IN-PUBLICATION DATA

Masterson, Dan, 1934–
    All things, seen and unseen : poems : new and selected, 1967–1997 / Dan Masterson.
        p.   cm.
    ISBN 1-55728-485-7 (cloth : alk. paper). —
    ISBN 1-55728-486-5 (paper : alk. paper)
    I. Title.
PS3563.A834A79   1997
811'.54—DC21   97-34457
                                        CIP

IN DEDICATION

". . . aware of family time measured out like cloth."

```
            J           C
          D A N I E L   L
            N           A
      A G N E S         R
      R     T       M A R Y  J A N E
      T     A                I
      II    R O N   M
      U     T                S
C H A R L E S         H      T
            K A T H L E E N
                      E      P
      D A N I E L II       I      H
            N     J        G      E
      G E N E     S T E P H E N II
                  A        T
                           O
                           N
```

ACKNOWLEDGMENTS

The author is grateful to the editors of the following publications in which this volume's poems first appeared:

Back Door: "Leaving"; *Bergen Poets:* "After Three Days Alone"; *Black Warrior Review:* "Rescue"; *Esprit:* "Laid Off," "The Woman in the Corner House"; *Esquire:* "Shrapnel"; *Georgia Review:* "The Survivors," "Fender Drumming"; *Gettysburg Review:* "Ballooning," "Last Days in Missolonghi"; *Hudson Review:* "Opening Doors"; *London Magazine:* "Jail-Bait"; *Massachusetts Review:* "Sunday Dinner"; *Memphis State Review:* "Fitz and the Gandy Dancers"; *New Yorker:* "For a Child Going Blind," "Calling Home"; *New Orleans Review:* "Cook-Out"; *North American Review:* "Getting Ready for Snow"; *North Atlantic Quarterly:* "Chow Chow"; *North Dakota Quarterly:* "White-Tail"; *Ontario Review:* "The Mandy Poem," "Bat"; *Paris Review:* "Whatever You Say, Henry"; *Ploughshares:* "Heron"; *Poetry:* "The Outing," "Safe Distance"; *Poetry Miscellany:* "Bloodline," "Final Arrangements at Lucca"; *Poetry Northwest:* "Blizzard," "Avalanche," "Under Cover of Darkness," "The End of Things," "Locked in the Icehouse"; *Prairie Schooner:* "The List," "Starting Over"; *Raccoon:* "The Tower"; *Sewanee Review:* "A Visit Home," "Joseph Severn Sketches Keats and Writes to Brown"; *Shenandoah:* "Legacy by Water"; *Southern Review:* "Connemara"; *Wordsmith:* "Winter Sleep"; *Yale Review:* "Treehouse"; *Yankee:* "The Fawn" (became opening sequence of "Rescue")

CONTENTS

On Earth As It Is

FOR A CHILD GOING BLIND

I have awakened her
When the sky was at its blackest,
All stars erased, no moon to speak of,
And led her down the front path
To our dock, where we'd swim to the raft,
Finding it by touch
Fifty or sixty strokes from shore.

And sit,
Listening to things, the movement of water
Around us drawing us closer, a hunched
Double knot of child and father
Hearing all there is to hear,
Close beneath bats who see without sight,
Whose hunger is fed by darkness.

The neighbors see her often in the woods,
On hands and knees, smoothing the moss
Where it spreads in the shade, marveling
At the tongues of birds, the stained petal
Of the dogwood, the vein of color
Skirting the edge of an upturned stone.

This morning she awoke to the first flash
Of the magnolia, and will save the petals
As they fall, their purpled lids
Curling white on the lawn;

We meant to tell her how the rainbows come,
How they close into shadows,
How we would be there nonetheless.
We meant to tell her before
They arrived at supper this evening,
Rimming everything in sight.

She wonders if we see them
Cupping the stars, the kitchen lamp,
Each other's face, and we say
We do.

THE SURVIVORS

I. CATHERINE ANNE HANLEY

They knew scarlet fever when they saw it,
And they saw it on her neck and arms,
Could feel it in the pulse she gave off
As she lay in fever on her bunk twisting
The blanket to her face, a headache
Wishing her back to Dublin, to her own
Bed, her own window where the breeze
Brought the garden inside.
In three days it would be her ears;
In a week she would let go
Of her fourth winter, her parents' faces
Blurring away, her sisters' eyes turning
Into stars as she eased out of pain,
Wrapped in their blankets, surrounded
By everything she'd touched, swirling
With her in a weighted sack, to the floor
Of the Atlantic.

II. JAMES EDWARD HANLEY

They were told to return to steerage
Where they belonged, but stayed,
The father's eyes ending any argument
On deck; a tanner by trade, his hands
Were mostly leather; the arms, massive
As country fence posts, curved
Around his family bent at the railing
In prayer.

In time, they asked for more blankets
And took the children below,
Where they lay broken in the first grief
They had ever known, their mother close
To the father, speaking in whisper,
Learning again that his strength was only
Partly his own.

III. LAURA MARIE HANLEY

The child's third night was fitful; at dawn
She awoke in chill; by noon the headaches
Began, the spots scattered themselves,
And the countrymen nearest her bunk
Turned their faces to the wall.

They were five days from shore; the hospital
Could save her; fresh vegetables and milk
Would be waiting, clean linen and gargles,
Warm baths and oils when the peeling began;
She was less frail than Catherine, older,
And had never been sick before.

IV. ELIZABETH CARROLL HANLEY

She would bring her daughter through;
After eight weeks of living in stench,
Eating like beggars, sleeping in straw,
They would be in America where Uncle Patrick
Held a parcel of land in their name.

She would see to it that Laura Marie would be
With them; she would wager her life on it;
Through day and night she stayed
With the child, keeping the others away,
Restricting her diet to soft foods, listening
To advice from the curious and bereaved
Until her own eyes burned, even when shut; her throat
Closed beyond words, and she lay back
On her bunk, rubbing away the strawberry rash
That was forming on her arms.

V. LIZA, MARY, AND KATE HANLEY

They stayed below with their father when the men
Took the others, the men in thick masks and gloves
Who said kind things to the stretchers they carried,
And told James to come back in six weeks, that all
Would be fine by then.

In three hours they were on land, walking ahead
Of him, trying not to fall down in the crowd,
Feeling his hands urging them on, steering them
Wherever the signs told him to go, his voice
Telling them all the things they wanted to hear.

A man with a badge gave them white cards to hang
On their coats; their common code, Han-14,
Would get them together if lost; on to the end

Of the ramp where doctors worked in rooms
With ceilings as far back as you could lean; a man
Just ahead had his card torn in half and chalk
Scrawled on his sleeve; they took him
Out a different door.

They held hands outside and followed their father
To the trains; once aboard, they felt sure of things
And fell asleep, leaving him to watch the buildings
Give way to trees; by morning, they were there.

VI. MRS. JAMES EDWARD HANLEY AND DAUGHTER

A prayerful six weeks passed slowly in the house
In upstate New York, but the time came to bring
The rest of his family home; he would travel alone,
Leaving Liza in charge, and Mary and Kate
Would obey her as they would their mother,
Or he would know the why of it.

The trip to Ward's Island was long, but he ran
The gravel road to the hospital, stopping
Out of breath at the desk to be told
The third floor office would have that sort
Of information; it did:

Two entries. December, 1850, six days apart:
        Cremated due to contagion
    Elizabeth Hanley, age thirty-four
    Laura Marie Hanley, age six

The road to the depot was spotted with snow,
His hands raw where he wrung them, each knuckle
White at the bone.

The last car was empty, its windows heavy with soot;
He saw trees hardened with ice, and a sky going grey
Without clouds. He pulled the shade to the sill.

SHRAPNEL

*("Out-patient 04066066 continues to experience
frequent nightmares concerning actual presence of
inoperable grenade fragments considered migrant and
minimal . . . surfacing particles have been removed
by patient without incident. Request for psychiatric
consultation granted.* DJM, Maj, Med; 16 My 71,
Con Gp II US *Army Corps; Dix.")*

He is barefoot in the creek again,
Wandering between his house and the next,
Not fully awake from dreams of grenades
Blown orange.

Clad in summer pajamas, he fondles himself
For slivers unable to rust as they rise
From the streams of his flesh: grey hairs
Refusing to bend.

He enters the tunnel beneath the road
And squats there; the cannon of his voice,
Reaching both flanks, commands the neighborhood
To take cover.

There are no replies from the ranks;
The years have covered them with grass grown wild
In memory.

His fingers continue their search, sensing movement
Within, and succeed at his left wrist

Where a steel pricker stands rigid
—A miniature soldier—the point of its bayonet
Piercing the skin for escape.

He draws at it with his teeth and feels it
Give way; with his prisoner pinched
Between finger and thumb, he crawls with the current
Toward light.

Caught in the death of his squad, leaving
Only the moon as a guide,
He questions his victim, frantic to learn
The invasion plans of those left behind
To drain his heart.

In the blur of morning, he watches his enemy
Twist once before curling dead
In the palm of his hand.

Giving him now to the stream, using a leaf as a pallet,
He kneels to the dead man's voyage.

COOK-OUT

I rise from the sun-deck
To enter the thicket
In search of a bouncing ball,
And find instead a grenade
Rolling toward a thatched hut.

And I go deep within it:
My eyes dropping to a sling,
Hung from criss-cross poles,
Supporting a child, sleeping
Above the settling ball.

The concussion blows the roof off
Like a puff of dandelion fuzz:
Gently, not to waken the infant
Wrapped in flame and floating
Slowly, head over heels through leaves.

I watch until he burns away in the sun.

BLIZZARD

The drift he slams into swallows the hood;
He rams the gearshift into reverse and listens
To the tires burning themselves bald, the wind
Sealing the road behind; there's no going back.

He turns off the ignition and laughs; already
Late for supper, he allots two hours for the plow
To make its way to this back road he took at whim,
Another test of his mettle; every day more proof
Piling up, giving him strength to go on,
Surviving on memory alone.

Forty, greying, he stuffs his pants cuffs inside
His socks, zips his jacket to the throat
And slips on his racing gloves, the leather
Matching his leftover tan as it shows through
The patterned holes; he steps out into the snow,
Knowing what to do:

The trunk opens easily, the tiny bulb giving
Light enough to work; he unscrews the spare tire
And lays it flat on the roof, talking to it,
Explaining what it must become, his pleasure
More proof helping to ward off the trace of panic
He knows drifts like a shadow at the edge of the road.

The sun visor breaks off neatly, making a scoop
To scatter the snow from the hood; he opens it
And unhooks the gas filter cup; he carries it off,
Chuckling, pleased, stumbling back to the dashboard
Where he shoves in the lighter and waits for it
To pop.

He pours the fuel on some crumpled paper and pokes
The orange-coiled lighter at the center of the tire,
Pulling back at the whoosh of flame; he controls
The fire: large enough to warm the inside of the car,
Small enough to conserve the burnables he has piled
On the front seat: glove compartment maps, credit card
Tissues, six or seven old lists, a driver's manual,
Last night's newspaper, and two man-sized kleenex
He stuffed in his pocket at home this morning.

Already proud, his lips twitch as he realizes
There are yards of cardboard lining any car's
Insides; he thinks of the look his insurance man
Will have on his straight-lipped face when he sees
The car in the morning, destroyed for salvation;
The papers will surely do a story, pictures, quotes.

He dismantles both headlights, leaving their wires
Attached, and props them in the snow, aimed skyward,
And gets back in the driver's seat, flicking them on:
High low off on, a perfect signaling system for any
Snowmobilers roaring drunk through virgin drifts
Laced with fence posts and abandoned jalopies.

He knows the papers will set his next move in bold
Type; off comes the oil filter, on goes the lubricant:
Face, hands, back of neck, deep into both ears,
Explaining aloud to tomorrow's reporters the need
For layers of oil, how vulnerable the hairless human

Ear is to chill, the fragile pink fading to swollen
Grey, yellowish white.

He sees a quarter-page photograph of himself,
In a ridiculous hospital gown, pillowed-up in bed,
Smiling faintly to his left; again the visor
Shoveling snow high against the wind, leaving only
His door open a crack to keep the lock from freezing;
Back inside he flicks on the dome light and breaks

The rearview mirror with pliers, close at the edge
So it splinters, giving him three thin blades
To strip the ceiling, allowing the tire's heat
To come in; he slashes holes in the back seat,
Enough for feet and hands, another for shoes
And socks; he waits until he warms, pleased
With everything he's done.

But he knows there must be more to do; he studies
Every inch of his room, trying for that extra touch
That will give the newspaper boys a headline,
A handle for a feature; he smiles and begins ripping,
Wielding the glass like a scalpel:

Floor mats, lining, seat covers, and fashions a suit
Of clothes: mittens and hat, scarf and shawl, pants,
Boots, all jammed full of seat stuffing, tied loose
With seat belts and shoelaces; he will explain he was
About to make a pair of snowglasses out of the back
Directional cups but they found him too soon.

He dresses and goes outside, removing his hand-guards
To feed the fire another slab of cardboard, recalling
The way he dropped envelopes by the dozen
Into the corner mailbox three weeks ago, almost late

But close enough for Christmas; close enough
Is the way he likes it, always has.

He refuses to look at his watch; he knows
It has all taken too long, clever but not clever
Enough to take up the slack between the car and plow;
He curses the driver perched on his stool in some
Two-bit diner, sipping coffee spoiled with milk,
A greasy doughnut ringing his finger, his boots
Running snow, puddles forming on the linoleum,
Streams wider than the shoelaces binding his leggings,
Twisting toward the door, urging him up and out.

He hears him brag on about the weather, the way
He blasts it off the roads, how he's beaten his own
Record already: only five back roads to go,
And the snow coming so fast he may forget about them
And start over from the beginning; no one in his
Right mind would travel those others on such a night
Anyhow.

He tastes a second cup of coffee hot in the back
Of his brain, trying to suck it down; he moves his eyes
To the rearview mirror, hoping he is wrong,
Planning to see the glaring lights of the plow picking
Him out of the night, but he sees only a few flakes of glass
Left on the flat tin backing.

He leaps within himself, remembering the car top,
Clawing the air toward the tire, finding its blaze
Dead, its ashes wet and done for; he gets back
In the front seat, turns the key hard to the right,
Hears a rattle, and remembers the hood wide open,
The motor, the battery covered with snow; he says
Nothing but takes the tire down from the roof

And puts it back in the trunk, still open, its snow
Swirling up at him.

He decides to leave the headlights where they are
And gets back inside, locking the door behind him;
Piece by piece by piece he pushes all the stuffing
He can find back into place, regretting the damage
He's done to the cushions and walls and ceiling.

He sits behind the wheel, and for the first time
Becomes aware of snow leaking in where the vent latch
Is gone; within the hour, frost starts forming
On his cheek, flakes fall on his left shoulder, the bulb
Overhead continues to fade.

With fingers strangely warm, he pulls the headlight knob
And lowers his foot to the pedal: on-off, on-off,
Imagining the beams changing their tilt
Somewhere beneath the snow.

JAIL-BAIT

Barebacked and handcuffed to a post
In the village square of another country,
He is about to be short-whipped a dozen times
As she stands with her father who insists
On pressing charges under Canadian law.

She looks younger than she did last night,
But older than the sixteen years he now knows her to be;
There is time to remember it all:

The swarming goldfish
Looking more like orange peels thrown by workers

Years before the quarry sprang a leak,
Filling itself to the brim, leaving a train
Loaded with rock to rust on its tracks
Now blurred far beneath the raft
Gone lopsided by his weight.

Before he was dry from his swim from shore,
She was lifting herself aboard, tanned and untouchable
As any goddess rising from the sea of a dream.
A fish nibbled at her toes, and he shared her surprise;
They propped their heads on their hands
And talked for the moment it takes to know
That there are no words.

Lying together in the dusk, he ran his hands
Through the water, teasing the fish, her fingers
Finding his, her arms wet still and warming, her back
Stretched like young leather, softly oiled,
Her legs straight out and inching toward his until
They gave heat the length of his body.

They slid from the raft and swam in silence
To the farthest rim where the pines had spent years
Preparing the shore.

He lifted her weight and laid her down at his side
To watch the fish pucker their mouths and turn
From his fingertips, her eyes explaining that she'd been
Where he wished to take her, and that she knew
He would make it seem that she'd never been there
Before.

The only way out was the way they had come,
Back across the dark water, talking unheard, alone,
The beach long empty of swimmers.

The squad car was perched like a cat in the dunes,
Hidden, until its white eyes opened a path in the sand.

Barebacked and cuffed to the post, he can see
That the short-whip, curled loose in the sheriff's hand,
Is as tan as her legs set off brown and bare
Against her father's creased white slacks.

THE TOWER

He has spent another night
Walking through waves of nausea,
Balancing the pain behind his eyes
To keep it from falling
Through the roof of his mouth
And out onto the rug,
Showing itself to be the walnut
He pictures growing
In a fold of his brain.

His coveralls will make him
A keeper of the grounds, intent
On doing battle once again
With the filthy brood of pigeons
That has called the height its own.

He will set up housekeeping in the air,
Above the campus, where the tower's view
Of Texas is grand and clean.

A footlocker, salvaged from a tour of duty
Still active in his mind, will contain
Provisions for the rest of his life:
Ammunition to last the day, rimmed

By canned meats and fruit
And a rolled towel standing white
Beside a spray deodorant.

In the shade given back by the wall,
He will lay three pistols, empty
And cracked open, next to a pair of rifles
Soothed in oil, their scopes hanging
Ready in leather sacks.

He will give what he has to give
To anyone in sight,
Completing the lives of fourteen strangers
And changing the color of August
For the dozens left to bleed.

When it is finished,
When his captors unfurl his towel
And wave it above his death,
He will join those dead as they rise
From their scarlet shadows
Toward a dream he sent his women to:

Where the broken bodies of mother and wife
Will mend themselves and drift in clouds,
Whispering their love for him,
Their fingers longing to soothe his brow
Still barbed in pain.

AT MIDNIGHT

He saw the cardinal,
Perched like a fist of blood,
Fall through his mind
To the ground

Where the girl's body
Worked with the wind
To form a curled drift
That kept the river
From rising to claim her.

She lay as though in bed,
One arm bent across her brow,
The moon shading her lips
And left shoulder.

Puffs of snow
Had settled on her eyes
Like gobs of cotton
Younger girls use
To shield their lids
At summer shores.

She was nude,
Save a stocking
The color of sun-tanned legs
Knotted
Around her neck
Much the way she might
Have worn a scarf.

Her hair
Flecked with night snow
Was frozen to the skin
Of a bulging root.

Kneeling to learn her face,
He found only frost, and rose
To dress her warm
In a garment of green branches.

THE OUTING

*"Newtown, Mass., April 20: Five women ranging
in age from 80 to 96 drowned this afternoon when
a driverless car rolled across a rest home lawn and
sank in Crystal Lake."*   —NEW YORK TIMES

It was more like a dream than an ending,
The lawn chairs adrift on the grass,
The elm trees parting politely
So that ladies kept waiting might pass
Before Bartlett returns from the pantry
Where he's won some affection at last.

They enter the lake without Bartlett,
And settle down in the sand;
The windows are closed, except Bartlett's,
The handle comes off in the hand,
And Bartlett goes right on romancing,
Knowing that they'll understand.

They sit as they sat as they waited
For Bartlett in fine livery
Who's taking them all Sunday driving
And bringing them back for tea,
But Bartlett has conquered some virtue
And lingers inside wistfully.

And now though he's diving to find them,
And even holds open the door,
There is little to say of his sorrow
As he floats them each back to the shore
Where the others have come to verandas
To see the five ladies once more.

RESCUE

A fondness for birch trees
Found her poised in a patch of shade
Where the wind stays broken
And the ground holds damp
In a lingering fog.

Her flared nostrils steamed
As each sound cleared itself
In her mind; it was here she learned
To live out the seasons, waking
In half-sleep to her own bleating,
Rising from the residue of a dream
That has her leaping a cliff,
Falling it seems forever before
Impaling herself on a branch,
Blood blowing like the rapids
That roared up at her, until she wakes
Unharmed, unsure of things, even
The grass where she lay.

It was no dream that brought him to her
In the midst of that frozen lake,
Four mongrels yelping from shore
Where they gave up the chase, the doe
Sprawled on the ice, her year-old blood
Leaking from a leg snapped in half
When she leaped for water and found it
Gone, landing on something harder
Than the paths she'd known through woods,
Her good legs spinning her crazily
Toward the center of things.

The ramshackle door made a raft of sorts,
And he skidded to her side, working a rope

For a noose; her sound was that of a child
Shaken in the night, the eyes stunned open
In disbelief, the voice rattling
Through the windpipe, stopping in time
To be garbled by the lips.

He told her things she had to know,
How the rope would seem too tight, how she
Would bound on home before the morning
Even spent itself away.

The noose settled about the neck and sent
A shudder down her back; he moved
As shadows move, his hand ungloved
And gliding toward the leg, tangled in rope,
To set it free, to let the tug-o-war begin.

But she had other plans, her eyes tight
On his, a new sound snorting from her throat,
Her lunge crashing short against the door,
Giving too much weight
For such a mild-wintered lake, and the world
Gave out beneath them.

It was then he knew he cared only
For himself, his wife on shore, his children
At the window, their grandmother talking
His death away from an earlier grief still
Thundering in her soul, his parents far
At home, their phone readying itself
To ring-in the news of his drowning;
Those friends feeling the Sunday air changed
About them, the reason less than an hour off.

All that, beyond reach, where he stood
Shoulder-deep in the shallow hole

Of a broken lake, climbing the brittle rim
Only to have it cave in, dunking him
As often as he tried into water colder
Than he ever imagined water to be, knowing
He would faint dead away in it, to sink
Where he had floated warm in the sun
Of past summers, alive as any man had ever been.

And then, as though in dream, he saw his wife
Closer than before, a rope in hand, the lake
Splintering beneath her, risking all she had
To risk, her eyes meeting his in prayer,
The rope whirring toward him, a neighbor lugging
A ladder, gambling his weight and age
On the groaning surface, the long pull to shore,
The doe left behind for those with boats
To axe their way and save her, only to find
Her needing more than they could give,
Hauling her past the crowd, to the inner edge
Of her woods to die, to take a single slug
Below the ear, her blood run out too far
To claim, the freeze too deep to thaw.

WHATEVER YOU SAY, HENRY

He feels the catheter as penis,
Is pleased with its sudden growth,
And goes to great lengths fondling
What he can't raise his head to see;
"Pinocchio" says I, and the urine
Trickles to its holding bag.

In a haze that won't describe itself,
He sees the bottles above his head
And wonders what good they do.

"Oil change" says I, and the drops
Fall to his arm and in.
"Smart Ass" says he. "You bet yours"
Says I, and the toes of one foot
Move the sheet in pleasure.

They like him here; like his bark,
The way he tells them why
They feel so smug, well enough
To baby him, reminding them
They'll be in a crib some day.
"Time's coming" says he.
"Whatever you say, Henry—whatever."

"Damn right" says he. Cancer or no,
He says it out: the chaplain on rounds,
Gold watch and fob and vest,
Comes puffing in to ask How-are-you-doing-
Today-Henry? "Dying, thank you" says he.
What-is-your-line-of-work-Henry?
"English professor" says he. Oh-I'd-
Better-watch-what-I-say, he says. "All
Self-conscious people say that" says he.
Well-have-a-nice-day, he says.
"Amen" says he.

He still has his own mustache, and wants
To know what the plastic one does. "Oxygen
Without the tent" she sings; "Enjoy it
Like a breath of spring."—"Awful" says he.
"Behave" she says. "Beat it" says he.
"Please leave for a while" she says;
"I want to do his bedsores."—"Live it up"
Says I. "Smart Ass" says he. "Yours,
At the moment" says I. "Bet yours" says he;
And she rolls him off his rubber ring.

The lounge is empty, the magazines
Older than a barbershop's; nothing
Changes, faces smile and frown, open
And close; gossip and death survive.

Now he is propped on his side, his rump
Healing in open air; the phone
Rings from Alaska; the voice is hard
To place, but her name makes the catheter
Jump on its hook. "She doesn't know"
Says he; "It's been years."—"I'll write her"
Says I. "Leave her be" says he. "Like hell"
Says I. He shakes his head
In mock dismay and sleeps in snow

For a matter of minutes, waking
In an old dream with three women naked
On a parched lawn, holding him down
In a shallow pine box; he's cold
And yelling for help. "Why
Wouldn't you come; where were you?"
"Right here; it's all right,
I'm right here." Again sleep, longer,
Deep enough to send me home.

Route 59 is slurred with rain, cars dead
Along the curbs; the stink of the ward
Hangs on.

The clock on the mantle clangs time
And again, the phone wakens the house,
A nurse talks from his room; he's confused,
Thinks he is lost, would I talk him
Back to sleep, do what I can.
"It'll be okay, Henry; it's just
A dream, like the box on the lawn;

The nurses will get you blankets
And tuck you in, get you more milk,
One of those whopping pills; let me talk
With her again; you'll sleep,
You'll see."—"My ass" says he.
"No thanks" says I; "I saw it this afternoon."

LEGACY BY WATER

He stands, greasing himself
For the hardest swim of his life,
The jar on a log, its cap
Fallen upside down in the sand,
Flicking splinters of sun
On the house, all but hidden
In the dunes, where his wife,
His son, his daughter lie drugged
From too much summer.

If they were to waken
To the quick licks of light
Playing on the walls,
They would find him hip-deep
In the sea, listening to the bell
Tolling from its buoy, marking
The first leg of his journey.

He turns and waves
To the empty windows, ignoring
The pain lumped hollow
Under his arm.

He takes a last look
Along the shore and sets out
Through water colder than the lakes

He grew up in, thicker somehow
And darker, even the sand,
Ribbed like a washboard,
Seems closer as it deepens,
His long arms churning the surface
As though he were back home
In the faculty pool, matching
Stroke for stroke with his office
Mate, far more than the game of it
Pushing them on to the tiles
And back, head over heels in turns,
Neither admitting to keeping score,
His record growing worse
During the last of winter
And all of spring.

He can't help looking back
And sees the roof silent and dry,
Its shingles shrunken now to one,
Suggesting the pace he has set
For himself; he slows and stops,
Allowing his legs to settle
Beneath him, the buoy in sight,
A few more football fields away.

He imagines throwing a pass
And watches it sail the distance
Before striking the bell, breaking
The steady beat of it, the gong
Making the water tremble;
He feels it across the shoulders
And down through the groin.

The water on his lips tastes
More like sweat than he remembers;

The mouthful he takes, the same
As the gargle he used as a kid;
He swirls it about
And spews it out like a whale,
Lying on his back, wishing already
For a glass of water; better yet:
Bourbon and water on the rocks,
All on a foam tray he could push
Ahead, all the way out.

He laughs aloud and takes
To sidestroking his way awhile,
Easy, almost like lying adrift
In his father's arms, learning
To float from his fears,
Knowing vaguely his need for water,
The clean full feeling he has
Whenever near it or in it.

With every pull of his hand
He can see the buoy,
Left hand passing its measure
Of water on to the right,
The right scooping it on to his feet,
Smooth and steady until
The boredom of it all starts
To get him, as it always did,
Those long hours
In the campus pool: lap
After lap, the lungs lasting
Longer than his patience.

In front of him are terns
Searching the waves for breakfast,
Diving straight into the sea,

Disappearing to rise empty, now
And then a fish small in their beaks,
Eating on the fly.

No boats returning yet,
No one insisting he climb aboard
And tell his tale of shipwreck
And survival, no one ready to believe
He could swim from shore.

On his back again, right, left,
Reaching far overhead and out,
Feet doing their work,
Leg muscles loose, no sign of cramps,
No fatigue; left, right, left,
Just like the old days
In the senior aquacade, the fancy moves
Showing style and endurance;
He tries them all: the glides,
The circle rolls, the egg beater,
Ending in the butterfly,
Both arms jacking him out
Of the water, his shoulders
Feeling the strain, too much,
The sockets grown rusty.

He treads water and finds the buoy,
Closer than he thought, and decides
To race the rest of the way;
One gulp of air and he's off,
Slap after slap, breathing
Only when breath is gone;
He gives it everything he's got
Left, glancing ahead,
Keeping his sightline,

The bell louder and cleaner
All the time; he glides
The last few feet
And touches the casing, barely
Able to hook his feet in the rings,
His fingers tight on the seam,
And squints back toward home.

He begins to shiver, convinced
He cannot return, that the change
In his marrow may never be known;
He hangs on and weeps, pronouncing
Over and over the names of those
Waking on shore without him.

He closes, at last, his eyes,
The taste of blood draining
From his gums, a trace welling
In his ears, almost
Aware of the bell tolling,
Softly tolling, as he slips
Back into the sea.

Those Who Trespass

GOING THE DISTANCE

The late June sun had come in the window
Over his mother's bed, and he used it
To make shadows on the wall, but they came out
Looking like ropes, tight twisted things,
Wrapped around themselves. He flicked
All ten fingers and closed them
Into fists, pressing knuckles to knuckles
Until they hurt, as they did
When he'd fight in the schoolyard.

They were big hands, like Grandfather Fitz's
He'd been told, the man long dead, whose sepia eyes
Never closed as they stared him down
From the opposite corner, the oval portrait
Leaning too close on its wire.

He knew he shouldn't look below the frame
At his sleeping mother, but he did,
Sometimes, and saw things. He did not
Enjoy seeing her nightgown hiked up
To her hips when the sheet slipped away
In the night. He wished he could yank it
Down, tuck it in, pin it tight
To the binding running around the mattress.

What he liked best was lying at first light,
Her long braid brown and inviting,
Almost touching the floor. But he grew

Afraid when once she half roused
And turned, a shoulder strap slack enough
To reveal a breast, the only one
He'd ever seen. He tried to remember
Nursing at it, wondering if he'd fondled
The braid as he fed, if she caressed
Him in his nakedness.

But then he'd shut his eyes and turn
To the wall, getting his face
As close to it as he could, his left hand
Strained and flat against the cool blue plaster.
Often, near morning, she would say things
In dream, and he would cover his ears and hum
Until he heard nothing at all.

And now, on this the last day
He'd ever have to spend in grammar school,
He lay awake in the room he'd always shared
With her, and thought about

His father far down the hall
In his chamber, his bothersome snoring
Muffled from Mother's delicate sleep,
His sister close on the other side
Of the wall, in the room he wanted
For himself. He shut off the alarm

Before it clanged and was relieved to find
His mother wrapped, tangled,
Only a big toe jutting out for air
In the narrow space between them.

Downstairs, he smeared a piece of bread
With apple butter and sat on the porch,

Remembering the summer morning his sister
Forced him to stay on the bottom step
While she repeated the lie of a woman
In a long black car who would soon be at the curb;
She would wear a black dress and gloves
And laced boots. She would take him away.

He licked the last of the apple butter
From his thumb and went off the back way,
Over the fence and down the path;
He was late and stopped to get
A scolding note from Sister Helena.

When the last of all bells rang for the day,
He opened his locker and stuck
His copy of *Ring Magazine* in his back pocket
And took the leftover bottle
Of ink to smash against the brick wall
Rising high over the rectory window, someone
Yelling, promising there'd be hell to pay,
Calling him by name but in a voice that knew
It was best to leave him alone.

At the end of the block,
He settled under a tree, the largest maple
On the Town Hall lawn; he thought
Of it as his own and came to it
On such days. He pulled
His magazine out and uncurled it, Billy Conn
On the cover, his cut-man taking the stool
Out of the corner, the ropes tight behind him,
Thick and twisted, wrapped in tape.

The idea hit him like a quick jab:
He could have a ring! The hardware store

Had clothesline. He slipped one inside his jacket
And paid for the other two. And then home.

No one was there, and he went to the cellar.
He undid the clotheslines and looped
The three ends around the first steel pole
That supported the main beams of the house.

And then the braiding: crossing the strands,
As he'd seen his mother do a thousand times
At her vanity, stopping
To straighten the snarls, to tighten
The loops; inch by inch it grew
From pole to pole: the top rope
Of his own ring, his own place,
The rope burns on his hands
Reminding him of the shadows on their wall
This morning, Grandfather's eyes,
His mother's long plaited hair
Half undone by sleep.

He wouldn't use tape; he wanted the strands
As they were. The last knot tied, he slapped
The rope and it almost sang back.
He went to a neutral corner and saw Billy Conn
Coming at him. He circled to his left
And kept away till the round was over.

He stepped out of the ring and did
Some shadowboxing near the washtubs,
Banging away at the air, talking himself
Into a frenzy, taking a few shots to the head,
The gut, moving away, jabbing, sticking,
Until he was soaking wet.

The faucet squeaked when he turned it
On full force, cold water drowning out
Everything, hands splashing it everywhere,
His shirt and slacks and undershorts
Peeled off, a bath towel stiff but dry
Hanging from its nail near the stairs.

Barefoot and naked,
He stepped back under the rope
To dry off in the ring, wrapping the towel
Tight at the waist, tucking it in,
Arms held overhead in victory.

And then the army cot, folded
Within reach, to be snapped open
And snugged up against the pole
Closest to the furnace, two full floors
Beneath Mother's bed.

He stretches out on the taut canvas,
His left arm across his face,
The right finding the braided rope,
Curling his fingers around it,
Tightening his grip, running it slowly
Out and back as far as he can, his mouth
Going dry as he feels the strands rise
And disappear in the palm of his hand.

THE END OF THINGS

Supper tonight was served by strangers
In a truckstop far from the kitchen sink
Where his mother stood watching him back out
Over gravel, too close to the oak he scraped

More than once on those late nights they warned
Him about. Perhaps he's had enough.

His room is fast becoming a shrine: clean linen,
Homework arranged near his books, fresh flowers
At the door, new pajamas folded at the pillow
He should come home to, and the lamp: its limp Christ,
With a 15-watt candle in his fist, nailed
To the window jamb.

The father wakens in the night and carries a drink
Upstairs to disturb the room. He feels the bed,
Empty in the half-light. He flicks off the lamp
And studies the shapes of his son's belongings,
Hoping to find things missing, but they are there.

The B-29 they built together
Holds on to the sky by a thumbtack the size
Of a button on a puffcoat, the one his son wore
The last time he saw him slamming out
Through the pantry, his answer cut off
By the banging of the door.

He needs another drink, but lies down
Instead, his head sinking in
Where his son's should be. In what approximates
Sleep, he hears a voice behind the bed.
He rouses to speak his name, to coax him back home,
But sunlight comes to wash it all away.

He scatters the homework and curses his wife
And her fastidious shrine. Downstairs
It is the same. No one will look at him. They know
He's been drinking. He leaves them alone
And goes off to his den, to his tall window,

THOSE WHO TRESPASS

His son behind the mower, the hedge
Fencing him in on three sides. But it is only
A tree moving in the snow.

He hears his wife and daughter in the hall,
Their quiet voices keeping the walls from falling in.
They shout Goodbye, and leave for the day.
He feels better already. He pours himself a drink
And heads for the yard, in search of kindling
Felled by the winds that worked all night. He sets
The empty glass at the edge of the woods and goes in.

Loaded to the chin, he comes to the front
Of the garage and lays a fire as his son would
Have it: twigs tangled like a bird's nest,
Sticks forming an open box, and narrow limbs
The size of rake handles to finish it off right
In the middle of the driveway.

Inside for a clean glass, bourbon, and ice.
And then the flame: the first strike does it.
The kitchen match goes white and orange and blue.
But he is gone, back inside,

Upstairs at the window, jamming the storm sash up
As far as it goes. And now it begins. Here come
The pillows and sheets and blanket. A shelf wrenched
From the closet wall. The straightback chair
Breaks when it hits the concrete. The desk
Is too big and takes the windowframe with it:
Glass and putty sailing like ice and snow.
The single mattress bounces when it hits. The box
Spring cracks once and falls on its side.

And now a wait while the rug is rolled
And lowered by its fringe.

Here, the pajamas unfolding. Homework flying
Like kites, books by the dozen flapping
To the ground. The model plane is off its tack,
Heading for the fire.

Drawers and their sweaters are on the way,
A closet floor of shoes and boots, shirts, jeans
By the armful, jackets and ties, two stereo speakers,
A double rack of albums, lacrosse sticks
And helmet, bedsides and headboards, a clock
Trailing its cord, a hockey stick and floor lamp
With shade still attached, a calendar
Turning its month over at last.

TREEHOUSE

He backs out the nails
But the railings hold fast, ingrown
On the tracks of a ruined oak
Rising half dead on the moonlit side
Of the lawn.

On a crisscross of scraps and tenpenny nails,
He finds the initials they carved without him
In the glare of a dimestore lantern
Long gone from the hook
That gives way at his touch.

He dismantles it all, piece by piece,
Sailing each hunk to the foot
Of the ladder strapped to the tree.

The roof has worn away;
Only a strip of canvas puckers along
Its hem of tacks; he takes them
One at a time.

Finished, he climbs down and sits
On the boulder he used to hope
They would miss
If they fell from their sleep.

He looks up at too many branches,
Too much sky, and begins
To do what he taught them to do
When they begged for a place
Of their own in the leaves.

He collects all the wood
He can hold and goes back up
To rebuild the past: each board
Falling into place, its nails returned
Without question.

At midnight, he unties the ladder
And lets it slide away to the ground;
He lies flat out, extending his arms
And legs, until he is touching
The trunks of four oaks,
Spread-eagle in the middle of the night.

LAID OFF

The woman behind the loan desk says No
For the last time and waits for him to leave.
He stands and makes sure his sleeve
Brushes against a stack of file folders,

Leaving a clutter of paper at her feet;
He doesn't look back.

Out on the steps, he hears the guard
Locking the doors behind him. Three o'clock.
He buttons the only button left on his coat
And straightens the paperclip he took
When her back was turned. He sticks it
In his collar, feeding it
Through the flap on the other side,
Twisting it back on itself,
Against the wind, before heading north
Along the tracks.

The rain has turned to sleet, and he looks
For a stopping place. A tavern roof rises close
To the roadbed, but he knows
He's not welcome there.

He takes the wad of deposit slips he stole
From the glass bin and lets it fly,
Dozens of giant flakes
Coming back in his face, a few settling off
To his left, dark down the sloping gravel
Where the stagnant water waits.

He's soaking through but can almost see
The tunnel beneath the interstate; if no one
Is there, he can get a few minutes rest.
It's no place to stay too long; beatings
Are as common as dogs.

He tries taking two ties at a time,
But settles for a shorter stride, squinting
His way to the underpass.

The walls are wet from seepage, but he's safe
From sleet. He squats on the foot-ledge
And pulls his arms close to his chest, blowing
Into one fist and then the other, his cheeks
Puffed and blotched, his toes working themselves
Like fingers in wet mittens, the girders
Rumbling overhead under the weight
Of holiday traffic leaving the city.
He's tempted to stay the night

But hears them in time to make a run for it,
Three toughs heading home for supper, shouting
Him out, swearing to take his shoes
The next time they catch him napping.

He stops beyond the bend and sits down
On the track, the same roadbed, the same
Water, blacker in the dusk. He hears
The train downtrack, the engine light closing in.

He decides to get out of the way in time
To watch the commuters
Dry behind glass. He feels for the largest stone
He can find, and holds it lightly, ready
To shatter a window, but lets it fall
Down the ravine, the caboose trailing
Its red lantern, pitching him back into darkness.

He sits on the rail trembling
Beneath him, the sleet becoming snow. He curls
Out his tongue, allowing flake
After flake to land and dissolve; others stay
Whole on his eyelids, closed against the sky.

He wishes he had gloves
And a pair of buckle boots—the ones

He had when he was growing up, when
His mother would turn them half inside out
To warm over the register;

He can feel the flannel lining, the gloves
Supple and light on his hands,
The new smell of leather
That means everything.

SAFE DISTANCE

(SD=300 x cube root of pounds explosive)

At seven thousand feet, the underpinnings of clouds
Look more like wind-ice on a mountain lake,
Its mist working among the curls, the sun
Slanting its shadows toward Canada, as his last day
On Earth opens its wings.

His leather envelope made it through the gate
With him; he holds it flat to his chest
As the 727 banks hard to the left, avoiding those
Who hurt him most; he leans back, aware
Of the headrest crinkling behind him; he wonders
Whether the night crew changed the paper
Or if he's deep in dandruff or Vitalis
Or the female breath of hair rinse
Ready to fill his nostrils if he turns; perhaps
A long blonde hair has already settled
In his own; he keeps his hands to himself & sees
The No Smoking sign still aglow; he smiles
Remembering his room

On West Seneca, the essentials laid out on the bed
Last night: upholstery thread tight on its spool,

The plastic spoon he licked clean yesterday
Afternoon, two baggies of black powder, the socks
They are flying in, & the ampule of mercuric
Fulminate that will blow them apart, but now waits
Cool in its cotton mesh, safe in a Parker pen
Whose sac of blue ink lies unplugged & limp
In a dresser drawer he will never open again.

His hands are on his lap, a scar
On one knuckle where a hacksaw jumped his grip
In his father's shop; it fades when he stretches it;
He makes it disappear again before tasting
The moisture forming on his palms: almost warm
Enough to detonate the ampule riding in his vest;
He tries to recall the doubting Thomas who left
A hand in Bomb School, but comes up with only half
A name; he folds his fingers into fists
& is bemused, thinking of them gone astray.

He will distribute them soon, the brochures,
Simple in design: xeroxed back-to-back after
Hours, folded once, black letters on yellow stock,
Elite type, precise language; they will read
How he learned as a boy in a cellar
That chemicals do what they say they do;
They will see the formula & wish themselves down
Behind trees or hillside where they might
Burrow & climb for their lives.

By paragraph twelve he'll be holding the pilots
At bay, having them squat at the cockpit walls,
Trying to find more distance from the ampule
They watch slide from its pen to be lashed
To the curve of the spoon, thread holding it open
& bare for the heat his fingers & thumb
Are frantic to give.

THOSE WHO TRESPASS

He wonders if some hero will make his move
& fail; the priest will mention Hellfire, a parent
Her child, a son his mother dying in Sunnyside;
Some will say nothing at all as they read
How the spoon will be laced to the baggies & stuffed
Overhead in the console
To melt all controls to their pinnings
When the ampule goes wild at his touch.

The cabin sign is off.
A stewardess is hustling drinks behind him.
He unbuckles himself & stands,
Adjusting the black powder socks that dangle
From his belt; he unzips the envelope & removes
The brochures; the stern man across the aisle
Accepts one & flicks on the overhead light.
It is 8:13; they are due at La Guardia at nine.

FITZ AND THE GANDY DANCERS

> (*The railroad track-laborer often appeared to be
> dancing as he'd swing and heave the tools of his trade,
> manufactured somewhat exclusively in Chicago by
> the now defunct Gandy Corporation.*)

His visits home are risings from the dead:
The walk down Woodward from the depot,
Kittie waiting at the doorstep, smoothing
The clean white apron she starched
And ironed an hour ago.

There's always the unwinding, the hiding away
Of the suitcase as though he were going
To stay, the toothbrush back in its circle

At the sink, the hairbrush upside down
On the shelf, the drapes thrown open
In the far bedroom, closed off when he's gone.

No matter the season, Fitz goes by himself
Alongside the barn to the stream he compares
To a mile of track west of Galeton, the same
Dips and turns. He prefers the stream,

But his crew's not there clearing the way
For the 9:53 from Buffalo, waving it on
Before heading out to fix whatever
It rattled loose
Between milepost #599 and #607.

There'll be joints in need of shims,
A dozen or more spikes riding up, a tie
Edging away from its stones; everything
Scrawled on a pad
They hand him at quitting time.

The stream is almost quiet. The rime
That flared the willow is gone, the beards
Of ice thinning along the crags, one more winter
Giving up to thaw; it's good

To be away from the gangshack awhile.
He spends too much time in it
Staring through window dust, thinking
Of his men, downtrack, taking a break,
Their tin cups in the canvas sack
Lashed to the handcar, the gallon of coffee
Tied thick with newspapers. He'd be with them
If he could, but there's no going back
From foreman to gandy.

Sunday night he'll be back at the inn
Sharing another meal with boarders
He'd rather see passing on a train,
And then the hours alone
Thinking letters he will never write:

To Lyle at dental school to ease up
On his work. To Kell at U.B. to lay off
The parties. And Kathleen
Spending the last year of high school
In an empty house with her mother.

A small shelf of ice gives way
At his feet. He watches it turn in place
And head downstream.

The night has come cold. He looks back
Toward the house and imagines Kittie
Calling him to bed, the patch of ice
Lost in the current some thirty ties away.

SUNDAY DINNER

Linen napkins, spotless from the wash, starched
And ironed, smelling like altar cloths. Olives
And radishes wet in cut glass, a steaming gravy bowl
Attached to its platter, an iridescent pitcher cold
With milk, the cream stirred in moments before.

The serving fork, black bone at the handle, capped
In steel, tines sharp as hatpins. Stuffed celery,
Cut in bite-sized bits, tomato juice flecked
With pepper, the vinegar cruet full to the stopper
Catching light from the chandelier.

Once-a-week corduroyed plates with yellow trim,
A huge mound of potatoes mashed and swirled.
Buttered corn, side salads topped with sliced tomatoes,
A tall stack of bread, a quarter-pound of butter
Warmed by its side. And chicken, falling off the bone:
Crisp skin baked sweet with ten-minute bastings.

Homemade pies, chocolate mints and puddings,
Coffee and graceful glasses of water, chipped ice
Clinking the rims.

Cashews in a silver scoop, the centerpiece a milkglass
Compote with caved-in sides, laced and hung
With grapes, apples, and oranges for the taking.

THE WOMAN IN THE CORNER HOUSE

Doesn't complain anymore
About her husband's late nights or drinking
Or, most especially, the way he left
His pajamas on the bathroom floor
When he'd come downstairs, freshly shaved
And showered, ready for his day
At the office where he died.

She used to wave goodbye through the oval
Front door, and trudge upstairs
To see if he'd remembered. She'd pick them up,
Wishing he were still in them, shaking
Them out, scolding him
In a voice no more than a whisper.

She'd fold them and tuck them
Under his pillow in the big double bed

They'd shared for thirty years in the room
Over the parlor and its piano.

She'd buy new ones once a year,
Grumbling about him
Right there in the men's department,
Deciding on a style that seemed young, never
Grey, usually without buttons, and always
Summer-weight and tall.

The pair she bought last Thursday had blue
Stripes. She had them gift-wrapped
In the store's silver foil and took them
Home where she left them
On the edge of the bed he'd slept in
For the last time a month ago.

After the local news and weather,
She locked the cellar door and left
The pantry bulb ablaze,
To keep the shadows in their place,
And went upstairs.

The bedside lamp shed light
On the box, waiting in its trim.
She opened it and took the pajamas
To her lap: the noisy sheet of tissue lost
Within the folds; sixteen more pins
To add to the scrap of flannel she kept
Tacked above the sewing machine.

She was pleased to find the inspection slips.
Number four had checked the bottoms; number
Twelve had seen to the tops.

He would have liked them. No buttons, bordered
Cuffs, four snaps on the fly, and enough room
In the seat to turn over
And over in his sleep.

His pillow was where it belonged.
She laid the pajamas full length along his side
Of the bed, the left leg bent at the knee,
Where she could feel it on her back, if he were there.

Come morning, she will drop them
On the bathroom floor on her way downstairs.

The neighbor children won't notice her
Waving from the door, but when the school bus leaves,
She will close the curtains and go back
Upstairs to find
What she knows she will find, and take them
In her arms.

AVALANCHE

She felt the snowfield break beneath her boots,
Heard the boom as the fracture spread eight, nine
Hundred yards left and right across the ridge.

She remembered to drop her poles and kick off
Her skis; she even tried swimming awhile,
But started to gag and rolled herself up,
Her face tight in her mittens, the roar
Working to cram her mouth and nostrils full of snow,
Half the mountain slamming downhill, uprooting
Trees, boulders, line-shacks, turning the night
Inside out, over and over again,

Until it all settled in the dark she felt
Coming to a stop around her. She remembers the chapter
On Fright and Self Control, and takes tiny helpings
Of air trapped in the space her mittens made.

She has no idea which way is up. It is
Darker in there than in the childhood dream
Where something white was always at the window.
Now, there is no window, only tons of snow
Packed hard against her, front and back,
Like king-sized mattresses piled high
For the storybook princess and the pea.

She must not pass out; she knows snow is porous
Enough to keep her alive, but can almost feel
The ice mask forming across her face, the breath's
Own handiwork of shallow sleep.

If she is to survive, she must now force saliva
Between her lips. If it heads for her chin, escape
Is above; if not, she may panic and die
Upside down by herself,
The acceleration of nerves, the state of being
Scared to death.

She lucks out. Up is up!
She tries to come out of her bend,
And feels the slightest give along the curve
Of her body. It could be an airspace. There are
Such things—some the size of root cellars: hard
Slabs of snow tumbled together like a house of cards.

She turns and finds she can move her head; leaning,
Digging with her elbow, she drops off
To the left, like falling out of bed.

She stands on a slanting floor in the blackest dark
She has ever been in. She begins
Feeling her way around her cell, and something
Flaps across her face. She grabs at it
And holds on, hoping it is still intact. It
Is the avalanche cord, orange and long, that unfurled
From its canister on impact
When she belly-flopped at the top of the mountain.
She is hooked to it and has to believe the other end
Is where it belongs: waving merrily above her grave.

They will find her soon, she is sure, headlamps flicking
Across the terrain; they will tug at her cord,
Signaling as they probe and dig. She continues along
The wall, getting the contour of the place.
There are alleyways everywhere, but they may be
Dead ends; besides, she wants her cord
To have all the slack it needs.

On the nearest block, she finds a tilted shelf
Of torn ice, beneath it: a frond of hemlock; she eases it
Out, hoping it is still attached, but it comes off
In her hand. She sets it aside and becomes aware
Of the fragrance filling the room.

She squats and closes her eyes, as if
She were in a forest after a good downhill run,
And thinks: Perhaps she can tunnel to a tree;
Perhaps there will be a door there, hinged
By elves. "Grendel," she says aloud. "Mab, Lizard
Leg, Horse Nettle."

But she has missed the password; nothing opens
Anywhere. She laughs at herself and shakes her head.
What to do. Her rucksack is gone, ripped off
Up top. She could use something to eat.

THOSE WHO TRESPASS

She has pockets everywhere, zippers, buttons, snaps,
But she comes up empty,
Except for car keys and a penlight
Dead on its chain.

She knows there is air for a day or more,
And remembers the boy in Norway buried for a week.
She wants to eat snow but doesn't want cramps.
She wants to dig but thinks of cave-ins.
She needs to scream but no one will hear.

It's high in her chest, something
Like the ache from running too hard too long
Before you run through it and out
The other side. She lets it come on.

It's as though she's been scolded and sent
To her room. She takes off her mittens and goes
To her knees to fill each with snow. "Bad girl,"
She says and hurls her mittens away, starting to sob
Only a little, mumbling frightened things.

And then the right foot. She stands
And stomps the snow, running her fingers up
The avalanche cord, still safe in the air
Where it hangs. "Mustn't pull. Good girl. Mustn't
Pull." And she starts
Reeling it in, an inch at a time, allowing
The orange ribbon to slip through the roof
Like a thread from her mother's hem,
Curling at her feet, the last of it fluttering
Across her face and down her arms.

She sits and finds the end of the cord. She puts it
To her thumb and starts rolling it up, 'round and 'round,
Neat as a pin it goes, a giant thimble growing

In the dark. But she tires of her game and crawls away
In a widening circle in search of the hemlock branch.
She buries her face in it and strips a handful
Of needles, rubbing them between her palms, inhaling
The sweet sticky smear she has made of herself.

She plants the rest of the branch upright
In the floor, and lies down to face it, patting
The snow, telling it things, crossing
And uncrossing her legs behind her.

She saw him arrive in a jumble of fire, a wee
Bit of a thing on the lowest limb. He wore
A green jerkin with hollow stone buttons and knickers
Puffed to the bands. She started to hum
To see if he'd dance in his circle of light,
And the jig that he did made her laugh in a giggle
Inside. She watched him kick at the base of the tree
And bark fell away from the door.

With his hat held aloft and a sweep of his arm,
He bade her Good Day and Come In. It was in half light
She climbed, hand over hand, the elf
Urging her on from behind; up, up
To the uppermost rung
To a four-legged chair and a window of sticks
Tied together with vines, and a view
Of the snowfield below.

They were there, starting the scuffline by moonlight,
Wands marking the turn where the ski pole appeared.
She is tired from climbing and wants to sleep;
She will call to them later, after they find
Whatever it is they lost.

A VISIT HOME

The bottom sweater button
Is in the next-to-bottom hole,
And his mother's fingers almost
Find it out, but climb instead
To the polished head of a brooch:
A maiden blushing to the left, hair
Falling across a shoulder
Bared in sunlight.

Something about the eyes tells her
She should know him, perhaps
The young man who brings her groceries
Or Father Sullivan
Dressed for a day off.

But no. The voice is more comfortable
Than that; it fits the neighborhood.
His hair is going grey; tanned,
He must spend time along the lake.
The eyes react
As her father's would: cut glass
Catching light

Shed by a flowered bulb in the ceiling
Where they stand stopped
In the upstairs hall, she
At her bedroom door; her married son
Nearer the guest room, a step away,
Dressed from the shower
Hardly used since he'd lived at home.

She'd like to have a towel
From the linen closet, one of the long

Fluffy ones they used to save for company,
And wrap it 'round his head, the way
His mother must have done
Before he grew so tall.

He seems familiar,
But she can't believe the name
He used for her.

She takes his arm
And turns his face up
Toward the light, as mothers do,
And finally asks the question:
Whose boy are you?

UNDER COVER OF DARKNESS

He's made the flight before,
But never in a wheelchair strapped
Back-to-back to the last seat in tourist,
Within earshot of a leggy stewardess
Complaining of a rough night in Cincinnati.

The secret he's kept in his abdomen
Feels like a loaf of bread swallowed whole,
Deep in its wraps of flesh and blankets, flexing
Its tendrils from hip to groin, sedatives
Cooling it down.

He's cold enough to be naked; sure enough
That he's going to explode
That he almost asks for help, but forces
Sleep instead. He wakens

To a sinking feeling that takes him aground.
And then a ride flat out
On a canvas litter whose wheels
Squeal through the carpeted tunnel,
Clearing the way to the terminal with its ceiling
Wide as a ballpark. Outdoors they hit
A wind worse than Lake Erie.

Up a rattly old ramp to a hospital van,
Complete with a wall of bottles and tubes
And a lanky bag of oxygen draped over its tank.

The trip from La Guardia
Reminds him of Verdun, the back roads,
The afternoon of forest patrol in the Argonne,
Birds escaping like soot in the sky, safe
From the low cloud of mustard gas sniffing
At his leggings, finding the sweat it needed
To bring him to his knees.

The volunteer at his side looks more
Like a street-sweeper, white coveralls baggy
As a clown's, but she knows what he needs
To hear: Deep-breathe when the pain comes;
Exhale it slowly away; Go limp at the bumps:
Potholes that could hold their own
In a minefield.

At dusk, they'd settle into the trenches,
Scraping hollows in the front wall, and sit
With the war behind them, heads to their knees,
Helmets tilted back in case
Shell fragments caught them off guard.
The thought makes him shudder,
And he looks at the bulb overhead, wishing
He could cup it in his hands.

THOSE WHO TRESPASS

She wants to help and assumes
It's a bother. She flicks it off, bringing
The night inside; he takes it in both
Eyes, adjusting to it, anxious to see out
The windows of the double back doors.

There are punctual bursts
Of arc-lamps, truckers flashing their brights
To pass, billboards lit up
For late commuters.

She is telling him what they will do
At the curb: the unlocking, the lift, the cold
Air and nurses waiting to lead him to a stall,
The questions they will ask. She warns him
Of the entryway: heaters jutting
From the tiles, an unearthly orange glow
Everywhere.

She is calling ahead, giving
Estimated arrival time; she spells his last name,
His first, and remembers the PH in Stephen.

The roads curve more in town, just as they did
In Verdun: three weeks in bed,
Pampered and groomed. This
Will be a shorter stay: The end of the line,
He says to the hand at his face.

The van stops, lurches once
In each direction. The motor runs on, feeding
Exhaust through the floorboards. She is up
From her jumpseat, putting a shoulder
To the door.

THOSE WHO TRESPASS

The blankets are olive drab to his chin.
Strangers take him up and out,
Held for a moment
On a rush of cold air
Before turning headfirst
Into a corridor of orange light.

OPENING DOORS

He remembered to ease back on the key
Before turning to the left. It clicked
Open and the tin weatherstripping creaked
As he stepped inside.

Something rushed over him; he went to his knees
And found himself making the sign of the cross:
Forehead, breastbone, shoulder, shoulder.
It was as though he'd tried to take a breath
Underwater. He stayed put

And pushed the door shut without looking
Back. He was staring at the red-ribbed chair
Where his father should be, the slippers
Under the footstool, a brown cardigan laid
Over the armrest for a moment
Three weeks ago. In front of him

Was the blanket his mother kept
On the davenport for the naps that gave her
Strength for lunch at the kitchen table.

The door swung in at his touch, settling
Against the side of the stove. There were dishes
In the drainer, and others left undone

From that last breakfast: two coffee cups
And saucers, a napkin folded at its place,
A plate whose toast was gone.

The door to the back hall was closed,
The skeleton key dangling on its rubberband
From the doorknob. He opened it a crack
And listened; the refrigerator hummed
At full blast. Inside, he saw a half loaf
Of bread, some eggs in the door-rack. Three
Covered bowls held leftovers from October.

The backdoor key was where it belonged,
On the cuphook near the dustpan. He took
The four steps down and started outside, but
Came back in and latched the storm door,
Leaving the other ajar. He went downstairs,
Flicking the switch with the jolt it always needed.

Near the furnace, beneath the bare bulb,
He took out the list. At the washtubs, he pulled
The lightstring and squatted at the hot-water
Tank, thumbing the dust from the dial.
He forced it left and heard the pop.

There were three shirts and a nightgown
On the clothesline that stretched to the fruitcellar.
He dragged his hand across them and turned
The handle of the door he'd helped build.
It needed an upward yank. The high window
Was black with paint, but the ceiling switch,
Once too high to reach, sent light across the shelves
Of canning jars, their rubber rings dried out
In open tins, pans, vases, trays, cardboard boxes
Wilting along the seams.

He took the stairs one at a time, almost
Starting to count them, but picked up a clothespin
Instead. He carried it to the landing and set it
Down on the top rim of the milkchute.

Out back, the garage door was locked, the key
Out of sight. The lawnmower was wrapped
In oily canvas, the patio chairs stacked
In the corner, the awning rolled, the chipped
White basin still half full of sand for grandchildren.

The red shovel, his own, there on its nail
For fifty years. He lowered the door
And headed for the house, wondering if anyone
Saw him, if he should wave.

On the sunporch, he opened the drapes
And attached a timer to the radio. Two others.
One for the floorlamp at the foot of the stairs,
And the last, the guest-room reading light.
New bulbs for both.

His parents' bedroom door was closed.
He wished he could keep it that way. Inside,
The gooseneck lamp was bent low over a saucer
With a spoon upside down in a dried puddle.
A small brown bottle stood close to its cap,
Its label toward the wall.
He made the bed and hung his father's robe
On the back of the closet door. The armoire

Was locked. The strongbox was safe
On the bottom shelf, its key in the sock drawer.
There was more than he'd supposed, but he took it
All, filling the suitcase with deeds and stocks,

Wills and bonds. He closed
The double doors and locked them.

He sat on the bed and started to give in
To everything around him, but shook it off
And went to his mother's side of the room. Things
Were in order. She'd probably stayed awake
That last night, tidying and sorting,
Vaguely agreeable, unaware she was walking
Through the house for the last time.

He could see the backyard from their window.
It was filling up with snow. He emptied both
Drawers of jewelry into a second suitcase and sat
On the bed. He lay back and let it come, all
The summer visits he'd spent there, the talks
With his father, the papers that would take over
At his death: what would become of Mother,
The house, the land.

There was a washcloth next to the sink
And he soaked it. He buried his face in it.
He wrung it out and took a towel
From the linen closet. He left the cloth to dry
On the edge of the tub and dropped the towel
Down the laundry chute,
Wondering what would become of it.

CALLING HOME

He dials his dead father's house,
Where timers go off at noon, at dusk,
At nine, allowing the gooseneck lamp
To come on in the den, the radio

To sift through the kitchen walls
And awaken the neighbor's dog,
Who no longer waits at the side door
For scraps.

Six rings—Mother
Would have answered by now,
But she's kept in a vest that is tied
To a chair in the rest home he chose
From a list when he was in town.

Twenty rings, and counting:
The pilot light flickers in the stove,
A cobweb undulates
Imperceptibly above the sink, the crystal
Stemware chimes in its breakfront.

He closes his eyes and listens.
He would like to say something,
But there is nowhere
To begin.

THOSE WHO TRESPASS

He'd find them among fallen limbs and brush
In the pitiful stretch of trees
They call their woods: stones the size
Of grapefruits, lugged out to the driveway
To be washed off with the garden hose
And left to bake on the blacktop
In the high sun before being tucked away
In the trunk of the car, along the sides,
Some down in the well, snug against the spare
Held fast by the stretch-strap doubling

As the tire-iron brace, a four-pronged plus sign
Looking more like a silver cross the way
It is propped, as though its Christ had fallen
Off, perhaps still there laid out
Among the stones

Headed for Buffalo, the outskirts,
The homestead where there were no rocks
To line the rose garden, houses no more
Than a car's width away from the next,
The narrow concrete tilting
Toward Bannigans' front porch.

And his parents would be there, pacing
The sunporch, waiting for the visit to begin:
Five days of clutter and talk, sleeping bags
And diapers, suitcases, books,
Hanging clothes, shopping bags; space enough
In the guest room.

And then the stones, last, always
Last: a few at a time; each placed
Ceremoniously along the rim of the rose garden
That curled against the side of the garage
To the back picket fence, turning left
At the Brodersons' shed and back
Toward the house.

Father is dead; Mother is gone, and soon
Strangers will be moving in. But the stones
Are still there, years of stones. Last night
He went off alone to do something about that.
He took only the three-inch paintbrush saved
From his father's workbench, one
Of a dozen washed after every use, never

To be thrown away, clean in its plastic pouch,
The snap still intact.

Seven hours by train, a short walk
To the Delaware bus, twenty minutes to the city
Line. He gets off a stop early and crosses
The street to the hardware store; the name
Has changed, common as a tenpenny nail.

He chooses a gallon of black enamel
And feels the plank floor shudder
Beneath him as the vibrator-stand
Shakes the can to a blur on the counter.

His mother's hands are shaking in her room, some
400 miles downstate; if she had lids on the cups
She would spill less tea on her sweaters and robe.
He may suggest it to the home.

Now, at 10:30 in the morning, she is saying
Her first rosary of the day, the floor nurse leading
Her on, bead by bead, as the paint slaps against its lid
Only a block away from the altar rail
Where she knelt for half a lifetime.

She doesn't know
What she is doing; she is seventeen again:
Springville, her brothers bringing her candies, Papa
Home on weekends from the railroad gang,
Her mother, rosary in hand at bedtime, and Kathleen
Sleeping with her own beads under her pillow,
The same rosary she holds in her grape-veined hands
This morning, a day's journey from where he stands
Waiting for his twenty-dollar bill to be broken.

She is alone for the first time in weeks;
The nurse has left to check on a noise in the hall,
And Mother goes on inventing melodies and words
To replace the orthodox prayers once her own.
In her wheelchair, the canvas waistband tight
As a saint's hairshirt, she feels
The beads loose in her hand. She fingers them,
Their roundness, small as pebbles, smaller
Than the stones her son has gone to see again.

She is drawn to the beads, sensing nourishment.
Her lips are moving in prayers
Never heard before; her tongue is extended, her eyes
Closed. She bends closer to the beads, accepting
Them now like the host safe in her mouth, sliding
Slowly as forgiveness on the same saliva
The aides dab away with tissues.

But now, it serves her well: for the beads
Have slipped fully beyond the lips; they could
Be green peas all in a row tumbling from a spoon,
Beginning their descent. No pain. No outcry;
She is deep in a tangled meditation; only
The crucifix is left dangling against her chin,
Its small silver link holding fast to the first
Of its fifty-nine beads.

Christ is in His diaper and the thorns are intact;
He is swaying slightly swaying, His features
Rubbed away by Mother's mothering. They retrieve
The rosary and dry it well enough
For her to go on to the next decade, the connected beads
Back where they belong: in the tiny palm
That waited like a cradle or a font
Or a crypt dark behind a large washed stone.

THOSE WHO TRESPASS

The paint can is freed from its shaking. He takes
The gallon as it is, swinging on its wire handle,
And drops the change in his side pocket.

The town seems almost the same: the village hall,
The playground at the corner, Kay's Drugstore
Bought out and revamped from counter
To name. The sun is hot as he turns down Lincoln
Boulevard. The house is vacant; he decides
Not to use the spare key for any last look.

The backyard is his grotto and he goes to it.
The stones are still in their looped line
Skirting the edge of the rose garden. He stands
Frozen in place. He wants all of the stones;
He wants to take them back to the ground he walks
Every evening, the frail run of trees
That flanks his house.

He feels for his rosary and finds it
In his suitcoat pocket, kept there for good luck.
He takes out the beads on barstools sometimes,
To fondle them in the dim light, saying
Their prayers half in a trance, and in churches
He needs to find when he is alone on the road,
Cities he doesn't want to see ever again.

The stones must stay. And so he begins:
Within minutes they are laid out
In a wide circle. Some of them tipping, a few
Already out of ranks, but each assigned a plot
Of ground: the Paternosters, the Aves,
The tenth Aves each doubling as a Gloria Patri.

The shrubbery encircling the yard is thick
Enough to hide him from the neighbors. He stands

At the back of the lawn, at the strand of beadstones
Which must stray from the others so that he
Might affix the crucifix-stone to its tip.
He knew back home which stone it must be:
The one with the purple vein running around
Its middle, and it is there.

He loosens the lid of the gallon
With the half-dollar he brought from his dresser
Drawer, the chifforobe which once stood
In his father's room and now holds his own socks
And shirts and bonds and bills. The paint
Is rich, the brush still soft; he can smell
The turpentine on the bristles, dry and stained
Deep with many colors far down in the base,
Each a different Saturday morning project done
With his father on this property, before the stones,
Before almost anything.

He kneels at the first stone and grabs too quickly,
Anxious to see the purple run of color, and jams
His thumb, blood forming already beneath the nail.
He replaces the stone and paints a rough cross
On it, trying to leave the vein purple
As a cinch for the stipe. He takes a giant step
To where the next stone lies: the paint
Goes on with hardly a trace of dirt; another
Step and he is past The Lord's Prayer, onto the first
Trio of Aves: the Hail Marys, one like the next.
The black is as lush as the counterman
Said it would be.

Another single bead, and he finds himself
Praying aloud, loud enough only for a stone
To hear. Another space and then on to the flat slab

Of sandstone he knew he would use
To connect the circle of decades. He gives it
Two brush strokes, unbroken,
A child's attempt at the ancient fish, good enough
For anyone who knows.

Three spaces beyond the fish lies a speckled stone;
It goes black, flush to the grass. Nine more
Go quickly, slopping the paint in a blob
On top, all at once, scampering back
And forth to smooth out the drippage, ripping away
The blades of grass
That are stained, stuffing them in his back pockets.
He says the prayers as he paints his way
Through the next ten; one has a bit of moss
From the shaded area along the spilloff spout
On the garage roof, the others bare
As the edge of grave markers.

It takes three Hail Marys to paint
A Hail Mary, the phrase "Blessed art thou among women,"
The line that slows him down: he finds himself
Repeating it, remembering the pitchers
Of lemonade Mother would leave in the shade
With chipped ice and a tall glass when he
Would use the handmower on a hot day.

He is rubbing the grass now, the way
He did when he was a boy, after cutting it twice,
Once fence to drive and, again, from garden
To house. He would sit and sip from the sweating glass,
The grass, the smell, the silent creatures
He'd disturbed, all
Holier and cleaner than the wood trimming
The stations of the cross in the church a block away

Over the back fence. He runs his hand
Across the grass until it hits his leg
And wakes him to his task.

Decade two. The stones are dusty and pitted.
It all takes too long and he wonders
If the weather will hold. He crawls on
To The Lord's Prayer, three spaces away; he smiles
As he comes to the words "Those who trespass"
And looks over his shoulder toward a space
In the hedge, but knows that
What he is doing is his to do.

The third and fourth are almost too much.
The paint needs stirring, the brush is filled
With dirt; his time is running out. If
He were to show anyone a decade, it would not be
Either of these. The paint is too thick, the grass
Too black, the stone-face showing through too often.

He must finish and get away; he feels it
In his wrists and ankles. He wonders if he should
Have come at all. His thumb,
With its nailblood dried black, is numbing.
He needs to be home, close to his own
Ring of stones at the far end of the property
Where he can sit and poke at the mild fires
He builds there, feeding the flames
With twigs and branches fallen on their own,
The rocks large enough not to split from the heat,
High enough to contain the blaze.

But it is time now for his best work.
The paint goes on like cream, as thick
As the cream that came

In the bulb-topped bottles of the forties
That the milkman would leave in the back hall
During the war if Mother remembered to prop
The shirtcard cow in the window alongside
The sign for the iceman and breadman,

Smooth as the blade of grass he holds still
Between his lips, thin and slick, not a blade
To crush between thumbs
To make an unseemly noise, not one that would grow
In a back lot, but one like all the others
In this yard, planted by Father, tended
By Father, watered by Father at dusk while other lawns
Went to seed and crabgrass and weed no one
Could name. It tastes good and clean and cool.

And now it is done. The last beadrock black
As the pieces of coal he was allowed to pitch
Into the yawning furnace,
When Father would bank the fire,
At nine-thirty every night, so that they could awaken
In Lake Erie winters to heat
Rising from the floor grids.

He looks back at the house, up
At the window where the afternoon light
Is spreading its daily shadow across the corner
Of the small blue room he'd shared
With his mother.

He goes to his knees and puts the lid back
On the empty can. He wipes the brush across the label,
The brand name, the directions, the cautions,
Cleaning the bristles as best he can. He will
Finish the job as his father would have him do,

But not here; back home, at his own bench
In his own garage, where he belongs.

He slips the brush into its plastic sleeve
And drops it carefully into his inside suitcoat
Pocket and walks to the corner of the house
Where the same garbage cans wait hidden
Behind the spruce trees. He lowers the container
Far down inside the first and heads for the street;
He does not look back.

He has his wallet, his ticket home,
His father's brush. He is listening to the Angelus
Tolling from the parish belfry: six o'clock.
But there is something else, quieter than the bells
Calling the villagers to prayer, something
Closer. It is his mother's voice, restored,
The same voice that used to call to him
From the kitchen window; she is obeying the ringing
Of the bells; she is intoning the beads
He has left in her name beneath the Niagara sky:
The threat of rain diminished, a healing breeze
From the distant river
Drying the rocks where they lie.

World without End

HERON

Late August, and the pond is holding
The summer's heat close to shore
Where leaf-litter has begun to form;
Even out at the center of things
There are pockets of warmth
Deep beneath a canoe short-roped
To a slab of scrap iron heaved into place
Once again on a scrub-topped boulder
Barely covered by water.

The swimmer is up from his dive,
Settling flatout aside the makeshift anchor,
Far from the potbelly smoke
Drifting from his empty cabin losing
Itself in the high peaks
Of the Adirondacks, the noon sun
Drying him out full length.

He stands, then hunkers down
On the rock, rubbing himself hard
With open hands, his hair running
What feels like snowmelt down
Across his shoulders as he searches
The vacant sky, the disturbed water
Coming from the inlet.

It is another ending, the last
Swim of the season, the day

Before he takes his place
In the downstate office waiting
For his return, the long year
Ahead, only a small framed picture
On a desk: this place
He is trying not to leave.

Something low to the water comes fast,
Gliding, making its way toward the rock,
Dipping, leading the wind, arriving
Overhead too soon, stalling
The right wing to turn abruptly,
Tilting into the sun, circling the boulder
And its naked swimmer: little more
Than bones spattered with meat,
Bland and bunched, trying
To become part rock, part air.

It seems to stop, casting
A huge ragged cross in shadow, its
Body stretched, wings straining
Their six-foot span against the glare
Mostly gone except at the webbing of wings,
The connecting flesh, the membrane
Where the tertial feathers become
Scapular, and the swimmer

Sees through it, the translucent window
Of tissue, fascia wrinkled yet clear, light
Streaming through ligaments and veins, an arm's
Reach away, the hoarse guttural squawk
Leaving the mandibles, loose plumage emblazoned
With feathers long and ruffled, bald legs
Set rigid as a clean-plucked tail, unblinking
Eyes, caught in passing, a blur
Of underbelly, the crook of neck tucked

For flight, a single flex of wings
Lifting the Great Blue atop the wind,

Tipping the swimmer over the side, drawing
Him toward the shadow skimming off
To the shallows, sending him deep, his arms
Folded to his thighs like wings,
Legs rigid, feet fluttering him on
Through the reeds, hands coming forward
To pull him into the dark corridor
He is making, his chest closing
Like a bag of air caught in a fist;
Time left to rise into sunlight,
But the need slacking off as his face
Feels the slim stalks reaching
For the surface long unbroken, almost still.

BLOODLINE

Her son's back is leather; wet,
It becomes her father's
Russet brown, tanned by field weather
However it happened to turn;
It is the Seneca skin he kept hidden in cloth,
Like something passed on in shame.

For half her life, she has failed
To bring him back through her son; and again
She kneels at the hill of stones, watching
The boy in the pond below:

He is unaware of the workshirt she sees
Come up from the grave
To fit itself to his shoulders,
Giving itself to water, as his arms pump

Against stalks, cutting a path
Toward the opposite shore, long muscles,
Almost a man's, pacing themselves,
As the back goes bare, glistening with labor.

He comes up from water, trailing
A branch half his height, and slashes
The weeds as though they were there
Waiting to be harvested; her lips move,
Unseen, and he is gone,
Into the thicket, her hand near, stretched
Across the pond, selecting a tree
For its strength.

He climbs a clearing limb, and walks
Until it bends, filling his lungs
With sunlight, his shadow
Laid like cloth on the pond; he folds
Himself in half, and enters without sound,
Surfacing a long way from shore,
His gaunt face turning for air,
Its features more like her father's
Than before.

He will come with grain dripping off him
Like water, words tumbling out, a plea
To go with him to see the world he's found;
And she will go,
Always she will go, to follow his hands
And something akin to that other voice
Giving names to things growing at his feet:

The adder's-tongue and bloodroot, trailing
Arbutus, and ahead, bunch berries looking
Like fallen dogwoods, lady slippers
Near pulpits, Indian pipes white

Against the peat moss floor
Of an earlier spring
When her father found arrowheads and clover
In the open fields of her hidden life.

GETTING READY FOR SNOW

The cellar trunk opens to dust,
Its mothball breath unfolding with wools
Set there last spring when we felt
We might be sharing the last
Of our seasons together;
But now, a bonus of days.

The hooded jackets, their gloves
Supple enough to eat; deep in one pocket,
A kleenex, grey and untouchable
As a dead mouse found in the rafters.

Then come the leggings, harsh as wicker,
And boots ready for the back fields
Where toboggans run all winter,
And a forgotten helmet
Fitting no one this year.

Clothing done, we turn to outer things:
Gutters banked with leaves, the shed
Waiting to be stacked with wood.

Nothing so suits such a day
As the raised arm falling, making its mark
On the crack of any log, scattering slabs
Enough to warm the bones through
The given nights ahead.

AFTER THREE DAYS ALONE

There are trees enough
      For both her eyes
And sky enough
      To overflow this place;
Afloat, we'd arch as one
      And go so deep
I'd lose her there
      As though in sleep
Before we'd rise
      To find the sun
Within her hair
      Across her face.

Inside the shack
      There is no light
Just lanterns all in need of fuel;
      The canvas sack
Has lost its ice, all
      Food untouched and barely cool;
The bed against the darkest wall
      Will go unused again tonight.

LEAVING

Now it is time,
Before the weather goes sour;
We will take what we can:
A change of clothes, a few tools,
Your medicines.

There will be plenty to eat:
Nuts and berries, cattail roots,

Grasshoppers, minnows, grubs;
You'll be all right; you'll see.

Things will seem better
When we are on the move; for now,
Forget last night; remember
Only that we are here, alive,
Able to forage for ourselves;
That is more than we deserve.

Look at me; for my part,
I am sorry; I cannot say more.
If we are to leave, it must be now.
Come; don't make me go by myself.

CONNEMARA

In a field of stones,
The house is stone,
A chimney scant with twisted smoke,
Its roof's worn thatch long since assigned
To vagrant crows in search of things
That crawl or fly at dawn.

Inside the single room,
A man moves lightly in his chair,
Lays his palms across his eyes
And mumbles something to the rain
That's started up again.

He pulls the woolen lap-robe
To his chin and tastes the smouldering peat
That swirls at him, up from the hearth
Where shadows burnt the walls all night.

He wears the woolen suit and vest he wore
To market all those years. The shoes
Are dried beyond repair. The necktie
He'll be waked in dangles from a low beam
Overhead, its four-in-hand knot in place.

He knows no need to leave or stay,
But there's a spoon or two of tea left
In the jar somewhere behind him on a shelf,
He's sure, and a crust of bread, he thinks,
As well. There'll be no going out
This day.

BAT

Badly maligned, nearly
    Impossible to track until the search
        Is done, and then you appear
As if summoned, swooping from the settling dusk
    Or flexing what should be cardboard
        Wings on that shriveled mouse
            Body when we lift a slab
Of wood from under the cabin porch, peat
    Moss soft beneath your belly,
The hiss spitting out from triangled lips or beak
    Or whatever it is that leaves a check mark
        On a girl's cheekbone: a scold to stay out
Of deserted houses, to let your kind be, no brooms
    No sticks no shoes or baseball caps,
        Nothing but the edge
        Of this shovel held hard
            Against your neck, stopping
        The night air from being sucked in,

Puffed out, all this earth
Surrounding you scraped up aside
The hole we bury you in,
That tainted soil, rabid
Even if not, pushed in on your dried leather,
Cleaner dirt, then a flat stone,
Heavier than it needs to be, weighing you
Down where you belong, the sound
Of your warning set deep under our skulls, able
To wake us at whim, the sky ready to drop
Kin who can tangle themselves in our hair,
Screech our ears off at the roots, nothing
We learn changing our faith in your malevolent ways,
Our only blessing large in knowing
We are not in regions close
As northern Mexico where you would crave
Blood meals, your folded ears and tiny
Leaf-like nose close to a feeding-site, more often
Than not a barefoot sleeping man, his neck
Safe due to your fondness for feet, now
Where you hunch to scrape a feasting-wound,
Holding on lightly, unnoticed, your dark tongue
Lapping at the pad of a big toe.

SUDDEN ENCOUNTER

If there's no shoulder hump,
It's no grizzly; you've found yourself
A black bear, no matter what shade
Of glossy shag she's wearing this season.

If she goes for you: swatting the ground,
Snorting, blowing, roaring, moaning,

Just back off. Don't play dead. Don't
Climb a tree. Don't run for it.

If she hasn't charged but is there taking
A long look, you'd better throw a fit: flail
Your arms, twist and shout, bang some pans, do a
Dance, swat your heels, whistle, scream, honk and hoot.
Still there? Then bark
And shriek, sneeze, cough, gargle and gurgle, huff
And puff, snarl and roar, growl and bawl and bellow.
If she's gone, backtrack and head
For home, cracking the air
With all the racket you can muster.

But, if she charges and keeps on coming,
And you forgot to bring your .458 magnum
And 510-gr soft-point bullets, and you
Neglected to pack that handheld airhorn
From your 18-wheeler, and the capsaicin repellent
Spray is back home sitting on the windowsill
Like a teddybear, you'd better find a hardside shelter fast
Or settle in for an open-air bar fight. Get
Something: pots to clang in her ear, an axe or stout branch
For snout-bashing, a rock, a buck-knife; and let loose
Some noises. At least her teeth have no
Shearing blades like the neighbor's cat. Small

Comfort? Well, that's so. But give it to her
Good. Smack her up side the head. Get right up
In her face and give her what for, break some teeth,
Kick some butt, gouge an eyeball or two.
You might get lucky; she could up
And turn away, wander off. If not,
You'll never know the difference.

VERBATIM

Well, you've got your silky pocket mouse,
The pale kangaroo mouse, the wood
Mouse, the classic mosaic-tail mouse,
The hopping mouse, and the northern birch
Mouse. But this,
This is your basic house mouse.

Flat as a nickel pancake he came
Under the cabin door, avoiding walls
Secured with steel wool, window screening,
And 45 yards of hardware cloth. Finicky,
Compulsive, nearsighted, in search of cheese,
Soap, glue, goobers, chocolate, and tootsie
Rolls, he settled for plain old peanut butter
Painstakingly tangled in a foot
Of cotton-covered polyester button thread
Snag-tied to the lip of a snap-trap's pallet.

Now, good as dead, his legs in disarray,
The tiny teeth smeared with bait,
His unclosed eyes still give off a dying light
Despite the spring-sprung bar, neck high,
That took his breath away.

His kind have kept the trait
Their long-gone kin brought in from overseas
In 1543: an excretion rate of 50
Droppings every day,
300 spurts of urine in between. We salute
Them now in quick remorse and bury him
At sea, remembering to flush. Vowing
Better barricades, we do not set the trap,
But try for sleep, sensing guilt
May only bring us dreams of mountain
Quilts filling up with furry things.

STARTING OVER

Took two lynx out near Grayling yesterday,
Females. Three males over by Logan
And Devil's Paw. Used those padded legtraps
And rubber tethers; stopped all five cold.

Double your common housecat, long
As a yardstick slung with muscles, greytan
Scattered with spots, furry ruff,
Tufted ears tufted
Cheeks, black-tip tail.

Had to gunnysack them down to Yukon Air,
Gustafson crates, extra rods and straps
All around, Flight #37 to Albany,
Then on to Newcomb by van.

Haven't been any in those mountains
For a hundred years or more,
But they're back now, set free to roam
The high peaks of the park, safe
From bobcat and coyote, even the fisher,
That rarefied air not to their liking,
Leaving a bounty of snowshoe hare:

Fair game for five broad-footed cats
Ready for night duty, getting used
To eartags grown clean into wounds,
Mercury-tilt collars snug on their necks
Sending pulsing notes back to range stations,
Five fragile songs caught in midair
By those who gave them names
Like Jim and Howler and Q2.

Red pushpins are starting to dot
The hacking-map, six million acres
Filling the back wall, crowding the window
That lets the Adirondacks in—bare
And green, perfect cover
For their far-flung escapes, all alone,
Apart till spring, when Cearse and Tanya
Will choose den sites and wait
For the others to find them.

WHITE-TAIL

He doesn't expect anyone hushed,
High in the leaves, waiting
On the padded shelf of a tree-stand
Held fast to the softwood trunk
By straps and clamp-chains mailed
From catalogs whose pages crowd man's sleep.

He doesn't know they have given up
The 3-legged stools they used to squat on,
In a scramble of brush, a 30-aught-6
Laid out and oiled across woolen thighs.

He doesn't sense the telescopic lens
Selecting a point of entry on his side,
The slug moments away, as he chews the first
Of a dozen low-hanging limbs encircling
The scrape: the mating ground he intends
To last the season, rut scent leaking
From the glands along his face
As he rubs them hard against the pale wound
Of bark already healing from within.

The thud breaks him in half,
The impact full enough
To knock his antlers off at the crown,
To send them into air
Already spattered with quiet strands
Of lung blown fresh from a hole
A fist could fill, tissue settling
On the forest floor
Where he feels his lost breath
Sucking backward toward its source.

He cannot see the branch
They are wrenching from the tree
He is sprawled against, or feel it
Going in across his open mouth, a ritual
They use, a cleansing they believe; long
As a man's bent arm: spruce—the taste
He avoided even in the darkest winters
He'd survived along the ridge of Stony Kill.

CHOW CHOW

(Liontamer Bertha 11/6/77–4/28/88)

But now I lay you down to sleep, dead weight
In a grey blanket, across the same back seat
You'd take to on command and sit straight-legged,
Alert to drivers caught in double-takes of you.

Tonight, you are no more
Than a sack of leaves dry in my arms.
The wet cloth against your mouth will not
Coax your jaws apart. Only your mild
Exhausted breath tells us you are here,

Your head slack upon the lap that held you
As a pup, the soothing voice in concert
With the hand smoothing the coat it used
To groom. Your fur comes loose
In handfuls; it carries scents of sick wards,
Sour flesh unable to control itself.

The vet is waiting after hours.
The parking lot is dark. The slightest tug
Steers you toward the room of tiles, chrome,
And light. Again we lift your empty weight
And put you down. Just once you make a sound,
A yip, a breaking in the throat. We listen
To the verdict: strokes, cataracts closing
In, some dread thing growing deep inside.

To the end, you flag your tail, forward
On your back, the way it would have been in show.
We take you close and watch the plugged-in razor
Shave a patch into your paw. We feel your skullbone
Hard against our lips and say goodbye.

LOCKED IN THE ICEHOUSE

Nasty as an old cigar butt, he'd sit
On the loading dock, his nub-legged chair
At a tilt to the door, heels hooked
In the top rung, thirty ton of ice safe
In canvas tarps on the huge plank shelves
He'd built by himself two wars ago.

You could see his tongs on the nearest nail,
Hung open, about to swallow
The leather sheath and pear-handled ice pick

Stuck within reach of his chopping hand.
The rubber apron, caught on a grappling hook,
Sagged upside down on its belt.

The platform was edged in sheet metal;
Tire tubes, folded and cut,
Covered the corners. He'd squint at the sun
Burning through his torn-umbrella canopy
And wait for cars to turn down the alley, ready
To curse them if they did and damn them
If they didn't. Mostly they didn't.

Nobody missed him,
Until some neighbor's icebox went dry,
Way too late to save him from the last things
He ever saw. There's that Jamison Lock
& Plunger plate on the door: brass, bigger
Than a belt buckle, eight screws
Holding her on. Must have been his heart.
No windows to break out, tin walls,
Below freezing by a degree or two, and him
In a tee shirt and dungarees.

But you have to be in there, afraid
To come out for an hour or two, if you're going
To know what it's really like. Like when
You're nine years old and barefoot
And stealing ice shavings, and he comes in
But doesn't see you, maybe, and goes back out
And sits in his chair forever. That's cold.
Chain hoists and hooks
Dangling from the ceiling, your breath
Going white as cigarette smoke.

You had to wait
Until he came in for a fifty-pounder,

Way in the back with that pad of burlap
Over his shoulder. Then you ran for it.

The floor's all wet with splinters,
But he had boots. You could see them
When they carried him out. Dead as a doornail
Was the way one yardman put it. Hard as a rock
Was another. But colder than a mackerel
Seemed best, considering.

THE LIST

When he feels the night closing in,
Like a jacket a size too small, tilting
The ground, skewing the clouds outside
His condo window, he squeezes his eyes
Shut and plans chores, memorizing each detail
Like a spy with a scribbled note to swallow.

He pictures the mountain cabin
They could have saved from demolition and puts
Everything in his head on slow motion, moving
His fingers beneath the pillow
That won't bring sleep.

He could have driven there at first light
And begun: tarpaper, pungent and thick, spread
Out for tacking on the rough-hewn floor;
Each flathead tapped five times now
With his right forefinger, the sound coming up
Through the pillow, every nail adding
To the straight silver shine extending row
After row across the 30-foot length,
The 12-foot width. Up

He finds himself up, rising up
To the ceiling and beyond, seven rolls
Of tarpaper light as bedding in his arms,
Enough nails sprouting from his teeth
To ward off a nightmare of porcupine.

He steadies both feet against the footboard
And hears himself hammering overhead, dust
Filtering down on the covers, the pitched wood
Settling under the first layer of dark,
Overlapping seams, buckets of hot tar, hauled
From the fire he scratched in the bottom sheet,
Hauled to the roof to be spread smooth
As bedclothes would be without him, but he stays

Put, one leg wanting to curl away. He remains
Stiff-legged, knowing how to lie safe on a roof.
A hanging drop lands him on hands and knees,
Leaves and small sticks sticking to palms and arms
And dungarees; he looks like a scarecrow blown in
From the fields for lunch or a nap or a book
Of matches, or maybe to help in rolling out
The bottom run of tarpaper for the front wall.
The back, the sides, the front; he's done.

The cabin is wrapped, and he lays his hands
Flat under the pillow, the fingers moving on their own,
Unaware he is taking a break before going on
To the carpet. The knuckles are twitching
For sleep or action, but they have no choice
If the night is to be kept at bay.

It is indoor-outdoor rubber-backed weave
In the pattern he etched on his palm. It fits the room
Like a liner fits its drawer. The staple-gun bangs
In his ear but the pillow dulls the shots, pinning

The carpet edge to the floor; his sleeping wife
Stirs, only a slight break in her breathing.
He feels her close and goes on. Before he knows it,

The clapboards are stacked within reach,
The handsaw moving in his fist, bumping
The headboard, each cut precise, 7-hundred running
Feet ready to fall into place. He balances
The first over his head, high
Against the overhang, and whacks the protruding nails
Home, walking first to the left, then
Back to the right, pushing up and slamming in,
Board butted to board, all sides of the box
He could have saved and restored.

Inside, with bricks scoring his hands, he sets
And cements a 4-by-4 base and dances
The potbelly stove into place, leaving it
Firm on its four sculpted feet. Sheetrock goes up
With the flick of a wrist, the hard-asbestos
The same; chunks and chips from sawing ignite
Like a scarecrow's bookmatch and send rich wet
Smoke against the sky where clouds adjust the first
Slant of light enough to speckle the wall by his bed.

WINTER SLEEP

He hadn't meant to wander off or lose
The path the way he did, still warm, his coat
Unbuttoned to his belt, the work boots she
Had laced for him, a pair of canvas gloves
In case he found some kindling low enough
To snap, to stash beneath his arm the way
He used to do before he lost his grasp

On things, back when his words meant what he said.
And even now he tries a test but can
Not name the town his wife is visiting;
He shakes his head from side to side and squints
His eyes until the droning hollow note
He sometimes hears for hours at a time
Goes drifting off among the forest pines

He's owned for all these married forty years
But does not recognize. He tells himself
To start a circle-walk and all comes clear.
His broken gait goes wide until he finds
A trail. He hurries on his way until
He thinks he sees the cabin held against
Some unnamed day's last light. His throat is dry,

His legs are taking chill. He kicks the trip
Root waiting there; it snares him hard and sits
Him down, just slightly dazed, upon the ground.
He finds himself beside a hemlock trunk,
Its branches sagging heavy with their snow.
A remnant of a leash hangs close above
His head; it might not be the one they tied

Their springer spaniel to each afternoon
For naps, that same old dog who loved to take
On head-to-head most anything on fours
Until he took an antler deep in fur.
The leash's nail is halved by rust, its chain
Pulls free against his chest, a talisman
He fondles well before he shuts his eyes

To speak her name out loud and see her warm
And safe there in her mother's den, with tea
And danish pastry by the fire, attuned
To one another's world gone wrong, aware

Of family time that's measured out like cloth.
The leash is cold but gives him memory:
Good dog, here dog. Come on, he'd say, and Beau

Would go to him all dripping wet from yet
Another hunting-swim, or running drool
From racing through the brush, and ready now
To lie this close, his head between his paws,
Content to have a hand that's laid to rest
Upon his back. A winter sleep comes soon,
And change of breathing too, a shudder from

His dreams, if dreams still build their broken flame
Within a leather thong that's too long dead
And empty now. He stirs and knows he should
Be up and on his way, but can't begin
To tell himself the thing he ought to do,
So settles back against the tree and wants
The cabin that he sees, no more than half

A walk away, to be his own; the door
Is darkened oak, the wooden roof's thick ice
Recast beneath a bit of smoke still caught
Adrift without its stove and moving fast
Into a breeze becoming wind, large flakes
Of snow diminishing to salt. Across
The changing crust he sees the wood he could

Have stacked that way some other place or time.
It looks like theirs: a standing hardwood cord,
All split and covered with a tarp. If he'd
Disturb the pile enough he'd have a slant
Against the snow, a place to curl up in,
And rest his eyes and hands and shut away
The night whose sounds are staying in his head

Much longer than he thinks they should. If he
Could only see the upper window like
The one she's gone to in the past to watch
Him working down below, to wave and press
Her face against the glass. If she were there,
She'd see him here. She may have tried to phone.
If so, she's on the logging road by now.

She'd never leave him in the woods this far
From home. He whimpers to himself and vows
To stay awake until she comes. He hopes
She is all right. Not good to drive alone
This time of year at night. He'll be relieved
When she gets home. Mulled cider would be good.
And cheddar cheese shaved thin on homemade bread.

She should have left a light on for his sake.
He cannot see a window anywhere,
But thinks of how they'll stand there looking out,
The snow quite soft and quick in coming in.
The leash is gone and both his gloves, his hands
Are open at arm's length, allowing snow
To land upon his palms. He'll close them tight

When they are full; the snow's good packing, wet
Enough to throw. The night is very loud,
But he is taken by the woods, his hands,
The storm, the thought of all these trees they chose
To be with all these years. He looks into
The ground and then against the crowded air
And tastes the dark accumulation there.

New Poems

THE MANDY POEM

*"A Creek Indian woman, Mandy Simon, who has been
arrested nearly every week for public intoxication, was
sentenced Saturday to jail for 99 years and fined one
million dollars."* —THE DUNDEE OBSERVER,
Yates County, New York, 1915.

And they took her to the trainyard, wrists cuffed chin-high
To a ceiling bar screwed to the back seat of a roadster:
Driver, guard, and Sheriff Bailey on board, Bailey
Of the pink-white flesh, Bailey of the flabby arms,
Riding shotgun, running off at the mouth
Till they handed Mandy up to Matron Merrill, booked
To take her downstate to a 10 by 8 like the one
That let the winds in back at the lumberyard,
The dirt floor she swept for wages swirling grit
Up into her sleeping loft, across the open box
Of years of letters, the can of dollar bills
Wrapped and tied in sacking cloth, fat
On Bailey's butt by now. She'd get him, in time;
Plenty of time to enact the symbols she's carved
In roundabout about her wrist: (#) to capture,
(*) to put to death beneath a starry sky.

#*#*#*#*#*#*#*#*#*#*#*#*#*#*

In this cell, smaller even than the Everglade chickee
Hut she longs to see, she wears the black trousers
Of the tribe she left behind halfway through her teens,
The faded black-orange longshirt tucked in

And thonged at the crotch, the kind she used
To wear for ritual. No thatch roof, no
Skin-tight sleeping shelf here, only a torn-rim
Squat bucket, a pallet of damp straw, a bulb
Dangling in its high-grill sock. Three slabs
Of brown bread. A tin cup. Raw potatoes,
Broken carrots shoved in through the gimme slot.
And BJ, the night guard, breath worse than Bailey's,
Rough beard, slug hands, huge needs, and hard
Habits built on daily canings of Mandy's back
And thighs and buttocks. Foreplay that turns him
Horn-bug red across the skull, bald, save a tuft
Sprouting behind what's left of an ear: a clump
He fondles and tugs at in between visits to Mandy.

    # * # * # * # * # * # * # * # * # * # * # * # * # * # * #

She will not meet him eye to eye, no matter
Which way he lurches which way he jolts, but keeps
To her symbols: homemade amulets she fingers
As he spends his groaning time; she soars alone,
Beyond the body, into the Upper World, allowing it
To digest her far inside a dark Passage. She returns
To scratch his name and code with stone on stone
Above the door she curls against in fitful sleep: #-BJ-*
And deeper still #-BJ-* until they will not rub away.

    # * # * # * # * # * # * # * # * # * # * # * # * # * # * #

He eases back the bolt and slips inside her cell
To catch her safe asleep. She kicks him down
To size and binds his wrists with ribbons
From her braids in time to twist his bootstraps one
To one in knot before he wakes to jolting pain to see
The red-cloth Swatch she's laid across his heart:
The point of entry for the spoon she's honed scrape
By scrape, for days along the wall. The gag, the hood,
A tangled run of hemline take his breath away.

She strikes the floor fire into blaze and whispers
Everything that must be said in graceful tones:
The Pale Dirge Reprimand.   The Cloth   The Breath
The Skin   The Bone   The Blood   given up for those
Who will never see Mandy dancing here in dust barefoot,
Sewn into Raiments of orange-black sweeps that cast
Her into Vision Life: Mandy of the Sad Enclosure
Doing what must be done: Spooning deep
Into   Cloth and Breath   Skin and Bone   severing
The tethers of the jackal-man's heart,
Lifting it skewered from its shallow grave
To hold it dead against the flames that flick
Their tall shadows amongst the stones.

#*#*#*#*#*#*#*#*#*#*#*#*#*#*

BALLOONING

> *"We saw them contriving their own approach: spiders,*
> *small dusky spiders, vast numbers of them, perhaps a*
> *tenth of an inch in length, arriving as a cloud before us."*
>
> —CHARLES DARWIN, *aboard The Beagle,*
> 20 *miles off the coast of South America, 1832.*

Hatched in Bogota, spiderlings
By the hundred scramble
From the torn skin of their birthsac
Up to the tips of grass spikes,
Leafless shrubs, fence posts, whatever

Allows them to face the breeze,
To extend their legs, to tilt
Their abdomens up, up
Till the threads from their spinnerets
Are drawn out by currents of air

To stream in long filaments,
Releasing their infantile grasp on the Earth,
To be pulled off into flight
Below the coast of Buenaventura,
Charting a course due west
For Galapagos, far at sea, knowing
To climb their own tethers:

Agile-legged acrobats scurrying
Up and back, drawing in and reeling out
Their lines, controlling their passage,
Twelve yards of self-thread hurtling
With them, obeying only the wind's whim

Of downdraft, at last, tangling many
On the great ship's luff and leech,
Jibsheet and halyard, even
The deadeyes and their shrouds, landing
Others softly on deck to be studied

In awe before lifting off again, swept
By a westerly, leaving only a few
Dozen stragglers behind: mere specks,
Picks of broken buttons trailing
Their knotless threads in blank light.

JACKDAWS AT THOOR BALLYLEE

Three miles from Gort, below
The falls of the Cloon River,
A wind-throw of hardwoods takes
The storm down to half of what it
Needs to turn the jackdaws inside
Out and hurl them flat against
The tower wall waiting ahead

In the sodden dark, their
Circadian rhythm ending
A late daystart early, sending
Them off to hedge-hop their way
Close to reedbeds in this rain,
Following contours astern
To others whose movements make
Them safer from predators
In such weather, but the weak
Are battered down to bruising
Shelter in some broken place,
Their impaired plumage drowning
Any chance of reaching the wall,
While flyers gain the parapet,
Entering the common slats
Edging the staircase of flatstones,
Thick highmounds of nesting-dung:
A steaming resting place, seven
Feet thick, dozens of wings
Folding in halftorn sleep, quiet
As the toppled graves dotting
The earthline beneath them.

JOSEPH SEVERN SKETCHES KEATS AND WRITES TO BROWN

*"Not a moment can I be away; he has just fallen asleep,
the first in 8 nights. A deadly sweat is on him."*

—*January 28, 1821*

From the piazza fountain, an endless fall.
Fanny's carnelian is always in his hand;
He will not have it set aside, occasioning
A restless sleep, but sleep nonetheless.
The chattering of his teeth slackens with his jaw;

The ghastly white has spread to hollows
Where the eyelids droop, the transparent skin
Taut across cheekbones and nose. First light
Will stun the eyes open, hazel eyes growing
As the face drains gaunt and gray.

The hair will not stay dry, and toweling
Merely rearranges pain into other pain.
The lips would take water, but he'd wake
With movement of my chair and be lost
Again in all his bad symptoms.

Hearing words read aloud seems pleasing:
Taylor's *Holy Dying*, the novels of Edgeworth;
And when I take to the piano, he asks,
Often, for Haydn, delighting in the childlike
Invention, losing himself in the distant melodies
That filled the sleeping-halls at Enfield.

I need only look away for him to end it all
With the laudanum he keeps at tableside: "How
Long is this posthumous life of mine to last?"
I will have the phial taken away come morning.
The relay candle is almost down; soon the thread
Will carry flame to its mate, setting it ablaze.
Some other dawn will see all these belongings
Torched, according to the Roman law of contagion.

He reads no more, cannot take up a page
On his own. You are on a list of eighteen
Who will share the volumes we intend to save
From fire, smuggled out before the room
Is sealed in quarantine. Doctor Clark speaks
To me of weeks or days. There will be turfs
Of daisies on the grave. A man awaits
To take casts of face and hand and foot.

There, his face is on the page, stopped
From its decline: an aura not unlike
The profile turning toward my voice; it is
Something he brings back from troubled sleep,
Something he speaks of only with his eyes.
Would that there were medicines,
As there are leads, to save such a man
From slipping away.

FINAL ARRANGEMENTS AT LUCCA— AUGUST 14, 1822

> *"The first body . . . was undoubtedly Shelley's; the tall,*
> *slight figure, the jacket, the volume of Sophocles in one*
> *pocket, and of Keats in the other, identified him."*
>
> —N. I. WHITE

They dress him in his burning white
And knot his cuffs with gauze;
The wine and spice across the sash
Improve the air he fills
Beside the empty grave
Trelawny placed him in a month ago;
Its legal mix of quicklime, now exhumed,
Blows itself to dust
Along the ragged shore
Here beside the sea Ligurian.

Trelawny and the Tuscan guard assemble all
The hooks and pins it takes
To hold the sheets of iron to the wind
And hold what once was Shelley
Rigid to the rack, to bring him down
To ash again.

Laid now inside the firebox, he's still
The driftwood he became, tumbling
At sea eleven days, drying to summer fuel
For this, his own, crematorium.

Lord Byron kneels apart in dread
While kindling-sacks are sopped with oil,
But comes to life in time to help
Arrange a wagonload of logs
Beneath the funeral pyre;
The clumsy banging of the furnace-tray
Gives thunder to the afternoon.

Trelawny sets the bundle-torch
And lays it to his friend, while Byron
Staggers off to crawl frantic
Through the friendless waves, to board
The anchored Bolivar, leaving Hunt
Still carriaged far behind,
His curtains drawn to shade,
To better comprehend the flames gone brutal
In their rage, the oven walls
A white hot mist as seen on casements
At Leman where splendid talk and firelight
Kept Shelley raving on till dawn
Within the villa where life seemed long.

At dusk, the sergeant leaves his post
Assured that quarantine's intact; Trelawny
Pries the lid-shield off and sees
What would not be consumed:
The soul's pulse left behind: the heart,
The heart, petrified—he scoops it out
And though blisters rise like landscape,
He will not drop it to the sand,

But moves back toward the sea
From whence it came, chanting
The single trochee of his name, the relic
Cooling in the mausoleum of his hand.

LAST DAYS IN MISSOLONGHI

> *"One request I make of you. Let not my body be hacked*
> *or sent to England."*   —LORD BYRON, *April 14, 1824*

A last breath, and the hacking begins.
The chisel, mallet, and Closky saw;
A blade, a probe, a common pick used cold
From the autopsy sack. And the last
Thirsty leech, fussed into place
Against the sternest vow, is taken back,
Leaving the temple and jaw heavy
With the slime of it now. A blood vial,
Full to the brim, is tipped into the drain.

The heart, the viscera, the brain gone vacant
In its skull, are set upon an ambry shelf
To be wrapped in curls of wool and stashed
Inside the cedar chips of a yawning coffin
Standing empty in the antehall, the tin
Lining flicking candlelight against itself,
A bill of lading, at the ready, lies open
On the sideboard, the cargo pre-listed
On *The Florida*'s manifest: one corpse,
English male; ten trunks: paper and cloth.

The lungs, floating like a diaphanous medusa,
Blue in a squat, sealed vase, will stay
Behind, a relic for San Spiridione.

The breathless cadaver, wrapped in winding
Sheets held fast to the casket's bedplate
With nailing-straps of leather, will slide
Into a cask to be filled at dockside
With six barrels of Wardsley spirits
For the five-week trek to the roadstead
Of the Downs in the Thames estuary
And the freshly turned soil of Newstead Abbey.

FENDER DRUMMING

The unused lot behind the mall is lit
Like noon by a circle of idling cars,
Their high-beams isolating two Dusters,
Dead center, parked grille to grille against
Their owners' shadows tilted up to watch
A coin disappear in a late August sky then
Reappear, inside a broad band of light, flip
Flopping to the gravelly dust that swirls
Between their boots. Heads it is,

And the one billed as Downtown spits
On the dime for not being tails, rakes
His fingers through his grey thick hair
And takes his place at the right front fender
Of the teenager's car, a fender left unwashed:
A thud of curved steel waiting tight and thick
And dull. He antes up

His 50 bucks: blood money he rolls
And sticks into the ridge crack, while
Across the hood, the other they all call
Kansas City kicks in his roll and peels away
A chamois to reveal a hand-tooled fender,

Its powder blue spilling over the edge
Where his fingers are busy fondling it,
Rubbing and stroking it, preparing it
For all the things he has in mind.

The others know the rules and leave
Their cars, hushed, pressing the doors shut,
To sit on their bumpers, leaning back, allowing
Their engine blocks to shudder through them,
Headlights free to do their job no more
Than ten strides away from the drummers
Already testing the metal: tapping and banging,
Riffing away, a run of triplets here, a ruffing
There, half-drags, flams and paradiddles,
Feeling each other out with low caliber shots
Delivered at point-blank range.

They stop and hold their hands up open
For inspection, proving they have no boot
Wax no epoxy no nu-skin no clear polish no
Thread-tape no polyethylene, nothing
But scars to keep their flesh from popping
On impact. And then the once-only passing
Of fingers behind the ears, across the brow,
Picking up any oil they can find, forcing
It deep into the finger pads they rub-up
Aside their ears, hearing the friction
Lessen as each skinprint starts to slicken.

They nod and KC hits the slap-clock perched
On the hood-drain, stepping back as Downtown
Whirls his fist high overhead, slamming it
Back down into the fender as though burying
A knife up to its hilt, leaving a crater
Round as a saucer and thrashes out his

Opening burst against its rim: a signature
Ostinato built to last: a flat-handed
Ratamacue, its 4-stroke ruffs chasing
The diddy-raks of lefts and rights, their
Accents all in line, letting it flick
Off into what sounds like a wrong turn
But brings him to a dark side street where
He plays mean, trashy shots slashing a foot
High without blood, laying down blisters
That ring true, smudging the crosstown
Rumors that he was easy: nothing more
Than a down and out ham-and-egger broken
By endless weeks on the summer circuit.

The alarm clangs and Kansas thumbs it back
To Start, using the top arc in offbeat
Only to sweep it aside with a triple
Chop and the 12-count pause the crowd knows
By name and chants across the gravel: Let
The cat out, Let the cat out, Let the cat out,
Now; and he's off, the fender swelling
On its struts as he knocks its brains out,
Whip-cracking licks coming from somewhere deep
Inside; doubled over, his cheek touching
The fender, he muffles some ruffstuff, his
Thighs easing in tight, the tingle surging up
Through his groin, his hands no more than blur
As he lays down an intimate rumble, a morendo
Delicate yet soaring from steel to paint to air,
As the slap-clock takes his time away.

Downtown sets the dial to 5 and takes
A deeper breath than he should need, turning
Toward his own car, tapping on the window
For the door to be unlocked. He gets inside
For who knows what behind all that tinted glass

Rolled up tight against the local wannabes
Who are running loose at halftime, banging
Each other's fenders to beat the band,

While Kansas City greets a curve of blackshirts
That keeps the fans at bay, except for a sleek
Young blonde who parts the crowd to drape a towel
Loose over his shoulders before sliding her hands
Down his arms in ritual: a kiss applied to the tip
Of each finger as he slides them splayed open
Across her lips, parted to allow her searching
Tongue to apply its healing balm;

KC stays put and shakes his hands, as if he's
Just washed them in a stream, before enclosing
Her face in them, drawing her close, spreading
The towel over their heads to disappear
Into a long hidden moment that is ruptured
By crackling thunder clearing the air
For three jagged strings of wet lightning
That send her away with all the others
Scrambling for their jalopies, the rat-a-tat,
Rat-a-tat, tat-tat-tat of the first plips
Of drizzle augmented by wiper blades slapping
Away in broken unison around the rim.

Time. And Downtown steps out bare-chested,
Wrapping his tee shirt in knots around his head,
The rack of his ribcage showing through
As he faces off in the growing storm for The
Give-and-Take. No clock. Set Ready Go,
And Downtown batters off his Blind Pig stutter
Step. KC hammers back a hand-butt pounding
Version of The Stumble Bomb answered in kind
By Downtown's own knuckle-knocking riff of Let
Me In echoed by a flathand read of KC's

Small-arms Fire: a frantic run of punishing
Half-drags, flams and rolls that Downtown
Duplicates as the skies pour it on, drawing

KC's healer back to his side, shaking
In a chill she can't define, as Downtown's
Car door opens and a woman, too old for such
Weather, steps out and joins him without taking
Her eyes from his hands that are running
Rudiments with KC, beat for beat: ruffs, rolls,
Paras and flams, ratams and trips and drags,
Ignoring the rivulets streaming candy apple red
With every slash they lay down: the women
Edging closer but trained to know their place
As split pads widen on each side of the hood:
Trigger fingers tearing wide open, stroke
After stroke after stroke flapping with less
Force against fenders dancing with thick
Needle-rain that scrims their hands and enshrouds
Their women who sense a final thunder.

WOOD

A hump-backed stretch of soil holds fast
To a fresh grave marker of black
Cherry scored by a woman's profile
Glistening in bas-relief.

A grandfatherly man hunkers
Beside it in the snow, carving
The wings of a thrush, wood chips
Fluttering from his knife
Into the dark chamber his thighs
Have made of the light.

And then he's up and gone, trudging off
Through drifted fields, reaching
His yard sooner than he should, deeply
Out of breath. He opens a cellar

Door, stomping his boots on the steps.
The rafter lights come flicking on
As he bellies-up to the bench:
A thick slab of ironwood back-edged
By a pantry row of sorted nails,
Their canning jars still bearing names
Of berry jams and plum preserves.

He touches one and then the next,
But at the third he falls to his knees,
His mouth locked open, his voice shut down.
He awakens stiff to discover
He's spent the night slumped beneath
The workbench, his back creased through
By a woodbox filled with scraps.

He finds his way to the parlour
And looks up at the portrait hanging
Over the fireplace, her smile
Almost breaking him down, but
He makes it to the mahogany
Door and swings it wide open, running
His finger around the gaping hole:
A raw cut-out of a Santa
Fe caboose waiting to be crowned.

In the hallway, he fondles the newel
Post. Off with its head! He pops it
From its socket and sits down
On the bottom step to hold it tight

Between his knees, sketching-in
A clown's face, remembering to add
Kathryn's smile-lines around the eyes.

And up he goes, along a winding
Staircase that is missing five steps
Worth of balusters, their clean-cut
Stubs rising from their canted oak.

He goes inside the first room
And sets the clown head down amongst
A clutter of toys fashioned
From the wood of the house:

Here, The-Cat-in-the-Hat rising
Fully carved from the white pine haunch
Of a Boston rocker. And there,
A proud buck flaunting its brass rack
Of antlers, free of coats and shawls.

The missing balusters are here: bars
Shining in place on a circus
Wagon, its door ajar, waiting
For a sideboard lion's paint to dry.
The gate-leg table has been gouged

Into a checkerboard replete
With chips sliced from kitchen chairlegs
Sanded to the touch. A stack
Of alphabet blocks towers over
A blue heron and a clock
Whose enamel hands have stopped time
At ten ten while a radish-red
Sled with wooden runners
Is kept in rein by leather holds.

But he is at the window now
Kneeling beside a life-sized child
Carved in infinite detail,
The flesh tone of his cheeks so fresh,
He will never know a sickbed.

Only his feet, disappearing
As they do, into the uncarved base,
Could hold him back, and his father
Must sense it as well, for he takes him
Up and hurries from the room.

The boy waits in the front seat,
While his father lays a long
Wooden tongue over the car's trailer
Hitch and tightens it down.

He revs the engine up and pulls
The old buckboard flatbed out
Of the barn, the slats straining
In their slots from the bulk
Of upstairs toys and hundreds more.

And then, he's in the woodshed and back
Lugging a dark container
Toward the house and disappears inside,
But not to stay. He comes, spilling
The last of the bucket's drippings
On the doorstep and strikes a match.

At the bottom of the drive, he pulls
To the side of the road and tilts his son
Back in his seat so that he can watch
The flames clearing the hilltop before

Heading off across the tracks
To park alongside a broken curb
Healing in the thickening snow.

He lays a stack of toys
On a rickety porch, balancing
The newel clown atop a wagon filled
With wooden stars, smile lines
Warming his hands. He hears
A bolt-lock sliding into place
As he heads back to the stockpile
To bring another armload
For the house next door, and the next:
An apparition bent against
The growing storm. And now they can't
Be seen: the man the boy the buckboard
The dooryards and the porches—nothing
But snow, hushed enveloping snow,
Covering the Earth
And all the air above it.

Caught in a Draft

JOURNAL ENTRY: "FINAL ARRANGEMENTS AT LUCCA"

OCT. 2ND: Decided to go to the seashore and recreate 1822 cremation of Shelley by burning his thumb-sized likeness I carved out of a wooden dowel last night. Took along a homemade crematorium I tin-snipped out of a Folger coffee can. Poked 13 vent holes in the top, attached skids on the bottom, & put two cotter pins on head of box, for towing.

Fashioned a simple catch-tray out of remnants from the can. Left home at 8:45, at tail-end of morning rush hour, for Sandy Hook, NJ, near Long Branch. Brought gauze, matches, b'day candle, splinter-kindling, teaspoon of wine (Taylor white), spices (sage, thyme, tarragon, cloves, bay: laurel).

Reached seaside at 9:30. Changed into boots, old dungarees, heavy sweaters, & headed for water. Also brought along a world atlas to chart where Shelley had sailed, drowned, & washed ashore that August, in relation to my position. Walked along the beach until I was clear of fishermen, & settled in amongst some heavy timbers that had washed ashore.

Here, facing the sea, I wrapped Shelley in white gauze, tied the ends in knot, & applied the wine & spices, allowing the laurel leaves to rest under him, a leaf beneath his head, recalling how he'd skipped through the marketplace with laurel in his hair, proclaiming himself a poet & wondering why the townspeople made fun of him.

Smoothed the sand, 43 steps from the water, & used the wax paper that had wrapped the Bauer & Black gauze as paper for the kindling. The ocean breeze blew out the first 3 matches, but then the fire raged quietly. Gathered driftwood & stripped slices from it with a buck-knife. Tried to shrink my focus, allowing the box to seem lifesize, & placed the box atop the fire.

The paint blistered off & the tin went from silver to black. The wooden corpse, gauze, wine, & spices began to sizzle & smoke through the roof vents, a pleasant odor. Burned for many minutes, since I kept adding toothpick-sized bits of wood no longer than the enclosed Shelley. Let the fire roar & went to the water's edge to check the map. Was pleased to discover that Lucca was almost in a straight line from where I stood!

Could smell the fire, now less pleasant, as though some of the driftwood had been treated with creosote. Searched for something I could use to pull the crematorium to the water, and found a square-headed nail, made a rope out of leftover gauze, & returned to Shelley.

Crawled backward along the sand, pulling the box to the water. Allowed the sea to cool the box before carrying it back to the burning site in the palm of my hand.

On the way, I saw an orange caterpillar being tumbled by the wind. Put him on my chest, where he hung on, & took him back to the grasses & let him go. Opened the crematorium to discover that Shelley had almost been destroyed. Strangely enough, a chunk of the wooden dowel was left, as though I had repeated Trelawny's discovery of his friend's heart petrified among the ashes, the relic that finally turned to ash in Mary Shelley's vanity drawer.

Wrapped the heartwood in gauze & stored it on the catch tray
inside the crematorium, & sat down to record these events.
If the poem works, this experience will be part of the reason.

—DM

ABOUT THE PHOTOGRAPH

JULY 4, 1899   The Flanagan home on Woodward Avenue, Springville, New York.

Upper Porch: Paul (Kell) Fitzpatrick, Kathleen Fitzpatrick (Dan Masterson's mother), Belle Fitzpatrick.

On Lawn: Minnie Flanagan, Liza Flanagan ("The Survivors"), Albert Flanagan (seated), Patrick Flanagan ("The Survivors"), Floss Fitzpatrick.

Lower Porch: Charles Flanagan (standing), Sadie Flanagan (seated), Kittie Flanagan Fitzpatrick (standing—Dan's grandmother).

Porch Stairs: Henry Flanagan, Lizzie Flanagan Fitzpatrick.

ABOUT THE AUTHOR

Dan Masterson directs the Poetry Writing and Screenwriting Workshops at the State University of New York's Rockland Community College campus and at Manhattanville College. The recipient of two Pushcart Prizes, The CCLM Fels Award, The Poetry Northwest Bullis Prize, and a Borestone Poetry Award, Masterson's publications have appeared in an eclectic array of journals and magazines including *The New Yorker, Poetry, The London Magazine, The Gettysburg Review, The Paris Review, Yankee, Ploughshares, Esquire, The Sewanee Review, Crazyhorse, The Ontario Review,* and *The Prairie Schooner.* Professor Masterson lives in Rockland County with his wife, Janet, who is a psychotherapist.